EVERYDAY
Wraps
BY KNIT PICKS

Copyright 2018 © Knit Picks

All rights reserved. This book or any portion thereof may not be reproduced or used in any manner whatsoever without the express written permission of the publisher except for the use of brief quotations in a book review.

Photography by Amy Setter

Printed in the United States of America

Second Printing, 2020

ISBN 978-1-62767-189-7

Versa Press, Inc
800-447-7829

www.versapress.com

CONTENTS

Alyce Scarf	5
Collarey Shawl	9
Duchess	13
Eclectic Electric Shawl	19
Flush Shawl	23
Fractal Shawl	27
Ilana Wrap	35
Iris Shawl	41
Joycejubilair	45
Junction Shawl	53
Koloreak	59
Stratosphere	63
West Bluff	69
Wild Vortex Shawl	75

ALYCE SCARF

by Ann L. Albe

FINISHED MEASUREMENTS
76" long x 14.5" deep, blocked

YARN
Knit Picks Stroll Gradient
(75% Superwash Merino Wool, 25% Nylon; 458 yards/100g): Stardust 27379, 1 skein

NEEDLES
US 4 (3.5mm) 24" circular needles, or size to obtain gauge

NOTIONS
Yarn Needle

GAUGE
20 sts and 36 rows=4" over one repeat of body pattern, blocked

For pattern support, contact
theknottingway@gmail.com

Notes:
The Alyce Scarf is clean, simple and just a little bit funky. Eyelet lace on one edge highlights the asymmetrical shape and the gradient colorway continually adds a new punch of color as it is knit. Repeating rows of garter and stockinette stitch make this pattern easy to learn.

DIRECTIONS

Set Up Rows
CO 5 sts.
Row 1 (RS): KFB, K to last 2 sts, K2tog.
Row 2 (WS): K1, P to last st, KFB.
Rep Rows 1-2 three more times, ending with a WS row. 9 sts.

First Column of Eyelet
Row 1 (RS): KFB, K to last 6 sts, YO, K2tog, K2, K2tog.
Row 2 (WS): K1, P to last st, KFB. 1 st inc.
Row 3: KFB, K to last 2 sts, K2tog.
Row 4: K1, P to last st, KFB. 1 st inc.
Rep Rows 1-4 once more. 13 sts.

Second Column of Eyelet
Row 1 (RS): KFB, K to last 10 sts, (YO, K2tog, K2) twice, K2tog.
Row 2 (WS): K1, P to last st, KFB. 1 st inc.
Row 3: KFB, K to last 2 sts, K2tog.
Row 4: K1, P to last st, KFB. 1 st inc.
Rep Rows 1-4 once more. 17 sts.

Third Column of Eyelet
Row 1 (RS): KFB, K to last 14 sts, (YO, K2tog, K2) 3 times, K2tog.
Row 2 (WS): K1, P to last st, KFB. 1 st inc.
Row 3: KFB, K to last 2 sts, K2tog.
Row 4: K1, P to last st, KFB. 1 st inc.
Rep Rows 1-4 once more. 21 sts.

Body Pattern
Row 1 (RS): KFB, P to last 17 sts, K3, (YO, K2tog, K2) 3 times, K2tog.
Row 2 (WS): K1, P to last st, KFB. 1 st inc.
Row 3: KFB, P to last 17 sts, K until 2 sts remain, K2tog.
Row 4: K1, P to last st, KFB. 1 st inc.
Row 5-8: Rep Rows 1-4 once more.
Row 9: KFB, K to last 14 sts, (YO, K2tog, K2) 3 times, K2tog.
Row 10: K1, P to last st, KFB. 1 st inc.
Row 11: KFB, K to last 2 sts, K2tog.
Row 12: K1, P to last st, KFB. 1 st inc.
Row 13: KFB, P to last 17 sts, K3, (YO, K2tog, K2) 3 times, K2tog.
Row 14: K1, P to last st, KFB. 1 st inc.
Row 15: KFB, P to last 17 sts, K to last 2 sts, K2tog.
Row 16: K1, P to last st, KFB. 1 st inc.
Row 17: KFB, K to last 14 sts, (YO, K2tog, K2) 3 times, K2tog.
Row 18: K1, P to last st, KFB. 1 st inc.
Row 19: KFB, K to last 2 sts, K2tog.
Row 20: K1, P to last st, KFB. 1 st inc.
Row 21: KFB, P to last 17 sts, K3, (YO, K2tog, K2) 3 times, K2tog.
Row 22: K1, P to last st, KFB. 1 st inc.
Row 23: KFB, P to last 17 sts, K to last 2 sts, K2tog.
Row 24: K1, P to last st, KFB. 1 st inc.
Row 25-32: Rep Rows 21-24 twice.
Row 33: KFB, K to last 14 sts, (YO, K2tog, K2) 3 times, K2tog.
Row 34: K1, P to last st, KFB. 1 st inc.
Row 35: KFB, K to last 2 sts, K2tog.
Row 36: K1, P to last st, KFB. 1 st inc.
Rep Rows 1-36 seven more times, or until you have reached desired length, ending on a WS row that does not immediately follow an eyelet row. BO loosely.

Finishing
Weave in ends, wash and block to diagram.

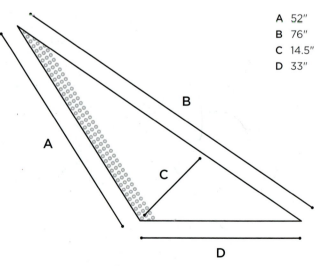

A 52"
B 76"
C 14.5"
D 33"

COLLAREY SHAWL

by Nadya Stallings

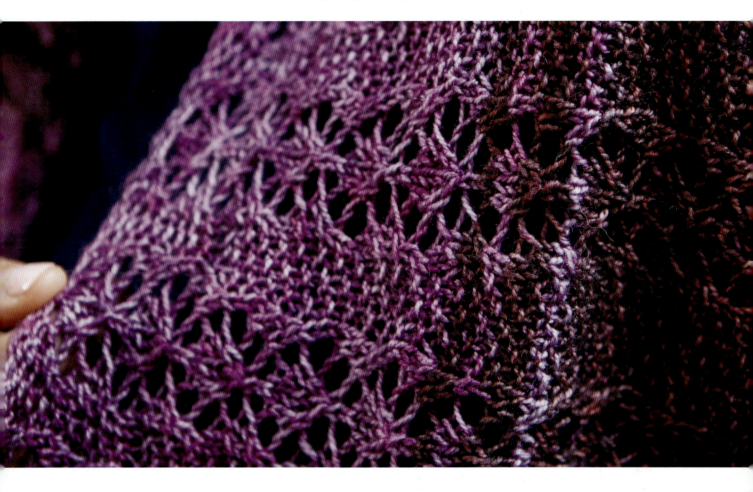

FINISHED MEASUREMENTS
38.75" top edge, 61" bottom edge, 10.75" deep

YARN
Knit Picks Hawthorne Tonal Hand Paint (80% Superwash Fine Highland Wool, 20% Polyamide (Nylon); 357 yards/100g): MC Ashland 27410, CC Eugene 27403, 1 skein each

NEEDLES
US 4 (3.5mm) circular needles, or size to obtain gauge
US 6 (4 mm) circular needles, or two sizes larger than size to obtain gauge

NOTIONS
Yarn needle

GAUGE
16 sts and 28 rows = 4" over Lace 1 stitch pattern with smaller needles, blocked

For pattern support, contact
nadyastallings@gmail.com

Notes:
This collar-like shaped shawl is worked as one piece from the top down with increases worked along two increase rows.

Lace 1 (worked flat over multiple of 8 plus 3 sts)
Row 1: K2, *K2tog, (K1, YO) twice, K1, SSK, K1, rep from * to last st, K1.
Row 2 and all WS rows: K1, *K1, P7, rep from * to last 2 sts, K2.
Row 3: K2, *K2tog, YO, K3, YO, SSK, K1, rep from * to last st, K1.
Row 5: K2, *K1, YO, SSK, K1, K2tog, YO, K2, rep from * to last st, K1.
Row 7: K2, *K2, YO, K3tog TBL, YO, K3, rep from * to last st, K1.
Rep Rows 1-8 for pattern.

Lace 2 (worked flat over multiple of 10 plus 3 sts)
Row 1: K2, *P1, K2tog, (K1, YO) twice, K1, SSK, P1, K1, rep from * to last st, K1.
Row 2 and all WS rows: P1, *K1, P9, rep from * to last 2 sts, K1, P1.
Row 3: K2, *P1, K2tog, YO, K3, YO, SSK, P1, K1, rep from * to last st, K1.
Row 5: K2, *P1, K1, YO, SSK, K1, K2tog, YO, K1, P1, K1, rep from * to last st, K1.
Row 7: K2, *P1, K2, YO, K3tog TBL, YO, K2, P1, K1, rep from * to last st, K1.
Work Rows 1-8 for pattern.

Lace 3 (worked flat over multiple of 12 plus 3 sts)
Row 1: K2, *P1, K1, K2tog, (K1, YO) twice, K1, SSK, K1, P1, K1, rep from * to last st, K1.
Row 2 and all WS rows: P1, *K1, P1, K1, P7, K1, P1, rep from * to last 2 sts, K1, P1.
Row 3: K2, *P1, K1, K2tog, YO, K3, YO, SSK, K1, P1, K1, rep from * to last st, K1.
Row 5: K2, *P1, K2, YO, SSK, K1, K2tog, YO, K2, P1, K1, rep from * to last st, K1.
Row 7: K2, *P1, K3, YO, K3tog TBL, YO, K3, P1, K1, rep from * to last st, K1.
Work Rows 1-8 for pattern.

If using the charts, read the chart RS rows (odd numbers) from right to left, and WS rows (even numbers) from left to right.

DIRECTIONS
With MC and larger size needle CO 155 sts.
Setup Row (WS): K all sts.
Switch to smaller size needles.
Rows 1-16: Work Lace 1 patt twice
Inc Row (RS): K2, *M1, K2tog, (K1, YO) twice, K1, SSK, M1, K1, rep from * to last st, K1. 193 sts.
Rows 17-24: Work Rows 2-8 of Lace 2 patt.
Rows 25-40: Work Lace 2 patt twice.
Switch to CC.
Inc Row (RS): K2, *P1, M1, K2tog, (K1, YO) twice, K1, SSK, M1, P1, K1, rep from * to last st, K1. 231 sts.
Row 42: Work Row 2 of Lace 3.
Switch to MC.
Rows 43-44: Work Rows 3-4 of Lace 3.
Switch to CC.
Rows 45-48: Work Rows 5-8 of Lace 3.
Switch to MC.
Rows 49-50: Work Rows 1-2 of Lace 3.
Switch to CC.
Rows 51-72: Work 22 more rows in Lace 3.
Switch to larger size needle.
Next Row (RS): K2, *P1, K1, rep from * to last st, K1

Rep this row one more time. BO loosely.

Finishing
Weave in ends, wash and block to measurements.

Lace Chart 1

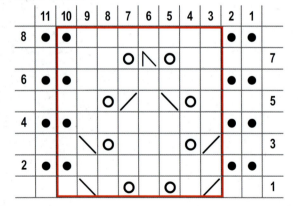

Lace Chart 2

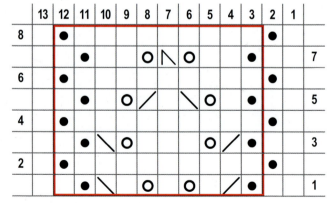

Legend

☐ **knit**
RS: knit stitch
WS: purl stitch

● **purl**
RS: purl stitch
WS: knit stitch

○ **yo**
Yarn Over

◿ **k2tog**
Knit two stitches together as one stitch

◺ **ssk**
Slip one stitch as if to knit. Slip another stitch as if to knit. Insert left-hand needle into front of these two stitches and knit them together.

◼ **k3tog tbl**
Knit three stitches together through back loops.

☐ **Pattern Repeat**

Lace Chart 3

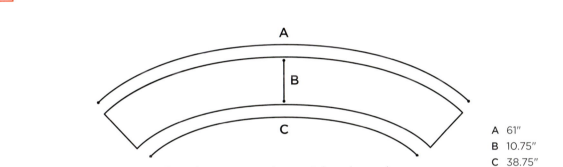

A 61"
B 10.75"
C 38.75"

Length measurements were taken along edge

DUCHESS
by Allison O'Mahony

FINISHED MEASUREMENTS
15" depth, 60" wingspan

YARN
Knit Picks Stroll
(75% Superwash Merino Wool, 25% Nylon; 231 yards/50g): C1 Hollyberry 27234, 2 balls

Knit Picks Stroll Tonal
(75% Superwash Merino Wool, 25% Nylon; 462 yards/100g): C2 Heartfelt 27079, 1 skein

NEEDLES
US 8 (5mm) one 40" circular needle, or size to obtain gauge

NOTIONS
Yarn Needle
Stitch Markers (2)

GAUGE
18 sts and 40 rows = 4" in Garter Stitch, blocked
18 sts and 32 rows = 4" in Lace Pattern, blocked

For pattern support, contact
allison@kniterations.ca

Notes:
Duchess is a garter stitch shawlette with a simple diamond lace pattern designed to show off the rich gemstone colours of both tonal and solid sock yarns. Duchess has just enough lace to keep things interesting without competing with the subtle colour changes.

Beginning with a garter tab cast on, the body is worked in garter stitch in the first colour. The second colour is joined a few rows before beginning the lace pattern, which includes alternating garter and stockinette stitch diamonds. The shawlette is finished with a garter stitch border in the first colour. The border forms subtle points that line up with the angles of the diamond lace.

Stitch Patterns are both written and charted. If following the charts, read the RS rows (odd numbers) from right to left, and WS rows (even numbers) from left to right. The exception to this is the Set Up Chart; this chart begins on a WS (odd number) and read left to right while the RS rows (even numbers) are read right to left.

Garter Tab Cast On
CO 3 sts. Knit 11 rows, knitting the first and last stitch of each row TBL. At the end of the last row, do not turn work. Rotate work clockwise 90 degrees. PU & K 5 sts along edge of work (1 st in each purl bump). Rotate work clockwise 90 degrees. PU & K 3 sts along CO edge. 11 sts.

Knitted Lace Bind Off
K2, insert left needle into front of 2 sts on right needle and K2tog. *K1, insert left needle into front of 2 sts on right needle and K2tog; rep from * to end. Pull yarn tail through remaining loop to finish.

Setup
Row 1 (WS): K1 TBL, K to the last st, K1 TBL. 11 sts.
Row 2 (RS): K1 TBL, K2, (M1L, K1) 3 times, (M1R, K1) 3 times, K1, K1 TBL. 17 sts.
Row 3: K1 TBL, K2, PM, M1L, K to last 3 sts, M1R, PM, K2, K1 TBL. 19 sts.

Garter Stitch
Row 1 (RS): K1 TBL, K2, SM, M1L, K1, M1L, K to last 4 sts, M1R, K1, M1R, SM, K2, K1 TBL. 4 sts inc.
Row 2 (WS): K1 TBL, K2, SM, M1L, K to M, M1R, SM, K2, K1 TBL. 2 sts inc.
Rep Rows 1-2 for pattern.

Lace
Row 1 (RS): K1 TBL, K2, SM, M1L, K1, M1L, SSK, *YO, K6, SSK; rep from * to last 5 sts, YO, (K1, M1R) twice, SM, K2, K1 TBL. 4 sts inc.
Row 2 (WS): K1 TBL, K2, SM, M1L, K4, P1, *K7, P1; rep from * to last 7 sts, K4, M1R, SM, K2, K1 TBL. 2 sts inc.
Row 3: K1 TBL, K2, SM, M1L, K1, M1L, K2, K2tog, YO, *SSK, YO, K4, K2tog, YO; rep from * to last 9 sts, SSK, YO, K3, M1R, K1, M1R, SM, K2, K1 TBL. 4 sts inc.
Row 4: K1 TBL, K2, SM, M1L, P1, K5, P2, *P1, K5, P2; rep from * to last 10 sts, P1, K5, P1, M1R, SM, K2, K1 TBL. 2 sts inc.
Row 5: K1 TBL, K2, SM, M1L, K1, M1L, SSK, YO, K2, K2tog, YO, K1, *K1, SSK, YO, K2, K2tog, YO, K1; rep from * to last 12 sts, K1, SSK, YO, K2, K2tog, YO, (K1, M1R) twice, SM, K2, K1 TBL. 4 sts inc.
Row 6: K1 TBL, K2, SM, M1L, P3, *P2, K3, P3; rep from * to last 5 sts, P2, M1R, SM, K2, K1 TBL. 2 sts inc.
Row 7: K1 TBL, K2, SM, M1L, K1, M1L, K2, *K2, SSK, YO, K2tog, YO, K2; rep from * to last 7 sts, K3, M1R, K1, M1R, SM, K2, K1 TBL. 4 sts inc.
Row 8: K1 TBL, K2, SM, M1L, P1, K1, P4, *P3, K1, P4; rep from * to last 8 sts, P3, K1, P1, M1R, SM, K2, K1 TBL. 2 sts inc.
Row 9: K1 TBL, K2, SM, M1L, K1, M1L, K2tog, YO, K3, *K3, K2tog, YO, K3; rep from * to last 10 sts, K3, K2tog, YO, (K1, M1R) twice, SM, K2, K1 TBL. 4 sts inc.
Row 10: K1 TBL, K2, SM, M1L, P1, *P3, K1, P4; rep from * to last 3 sts, M1R, SM, K2, K1 TBL. 2 sts inc.
Row 11: K1 TBL, K2, SM, M1L, K1, M1L, *K2, K2tog, YO, SSK, YO, K2; rep from * to last 5 sts, (K1, M1R) twice, SM, K2, K1 TBL. 4 sts inc.
Row 12: K1 TBL, K2, SM, M1L, K1, P3, *P2, K3, P3; rep from * to last 6 sts, P2, K1, M1R, SM, K2, K1 TBL. 2 sts inc.
Row 13: K1 TBL, K2, SM, M1L, K1, M1L, SSK, YO, K1, *K1, K2tog, YO, K2, SSK, YO, K1; rep from * to last 8 sts, K1, K2tog, YO, (K1, M1R) twice, SM, K2, K1 TBL. 4 sts inc.
Row 14: K1 TBL, K2, SM, M1L, K5, P2, *P1, K5, P2; rep from * to last 9 sts, P1, K5, M1R, SM, K2, K1 TBL. 2 sts inc.
Row 15: K1 TBL, K2, SM, M1L, K1, M1L, K4, SSK, YO; *K2tog, YO, K4, SSK, YO; rep from * to last 11 sts, K2tog, YO, K5, M1R, K1, M1R, SM, K2, K1 TBL. 4 sts inc.
Row 16: K1 TBL, K2, SM, M1L, K1, P1, *K7, P1; rep from * to last 4 sts, K1, M1R, SM, K2, K1 TBL. 2 sts inc.
Rep Rows 1-16 for pattern.

Edge
Row 1 (RS): K1 TBL, K2, SM, M1L, K1, M1L, K2, *K3, KFB twice, K3; rep from * to last 7 sts, K3, M1R, K1, M1R, SM, K2, K1 TBL. 467 sts.
Row 2 (WS): K1 TBL, K2, SM, M1L, K to M, M1R, SM, K2, K1 TBL. 469 sts.
Row 3: K1 TBL, K2, SM, M1L, K1, M1L, K5, *K4, KFB twice, K4; rep from * to last 10 sts, K6, M1L, K1, M1L, SM, K2, K1 TBL. 563 sts.
Row 4: Rep Row 2. 565 sts.
Row 5: K1 TBL, K2, SM, M1L, K1, M1L, K8, *K5, KFB twice, K5; rep from * to last 13 sts, K9, M1R, K1, M1R, SM, K2, K1 TBL. 659 sts.

DIRECTIONS

Setup
With C1, work the Garter Tab Cast On. 11 sts.

Work Rows 1-3 of Setup. 19 sts.

Garter Stitch Body
Work Rows 1 and 2 of Garter Stitch pattern a total 30 times. 199 sts. Cut C1.

Lace Border
Join C2 and work Rows 1-2 of Garter Stitch pattern twice. 211 stitches.

Begin working Lace pattern, repeating Rows 1-16 three times, then Row 1 once more. Work Row 2 of Garter Stitch pattern once, then works Row 1-2 of Garter Stitch pattern once. 367 stitches. Cut C2.

Garter Stitch Edging
Join C1 and work Rows 1-2 of Garter Stitch pattern once. 373 sts.

Work Rows 1-5 of Edge pattern. 659 sts. BO on the wrong side using the Knitted Lace Bind Off.

Finishing
Weave in ends and block to schematic measurements.

Setup Chart

	19	18	17	16	15	14	13	12	11	10	9	8	7	6	5	4	3	2	1
3	~	●	●	MR	●	●	●	●	●	●	●	●	●	●	●	ML	●	●	~
		B			MR		MR		MR		ML		ML		ML		B		2
1					~	●	●	●	●	●	●	●	●	●	~				

Garter Stitch Chart

	15	14	13	12	11	10	9	8	7	6	5	4	3	2	1
2	~	●	●	MR	●	●	●	●	●	●	●	ML	●	●	~
		B			MR		MR		ML		ML		B		1

Legend

knit
RS: knit stitch
WS: purl stitch

purl
RS: purl stitch
WS: knit stitch

yo
Yarn Over

k2tog
Knit two stitches together as one stitch

ssk
Slip one stitch as if to knit. Slip another stitch as if to knit. Insert left-hand needle into front of these two stitches and knit them together.

knit tbl
B — RS: Knit stitch through back loop
WS: Purl stitch through back loop

purl tbl
~ — RS: Purl stitch through back loop
WS: Knit stitch through back loop

kfb
Knit into the front and back of stitch

make one left
ML — RS: Pick up the bar between stitch just worked and the next stitch on needle, inserting left needle from front to back; purl through the backloop.
WS: Pick up the bar between stitch just worked and the next stitch on needle, inserting left needle from front to back; knit through the backloop.

make one right
MR — RS: Pick up the bar between stitch just worked and the next stitch on needle, inserting left needle from back to front; knit through the front loop.
WS: Pick up the bar between stitch just worked and the next stitch on needle, inserting left needle from back to front; purl through the front loop.

No Stitch

Pattern Repeat

Lace Chart

(chart image)

Edge Chart

(chart image)

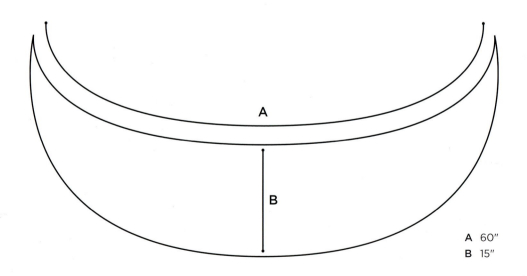

A 60"
B 15"

ECLECTIC ELECTRIC SHAWL

by Megan Dial

FINISHED MEASUREMENTS
70"x44" blocked

YARN
Knit Picks Stroll Fingering
(75% Superwash Merino Wool, 25% Nylon: 231 yards/50g): MC White 26082 3 balls, C1 Electric Blue 26406 1 ball, C2 Pucker 26401 1 ball, C3 Dandelion 25024 2 balls

NEEDLES
US 2 (3mm) 40" circular needle, or size to obtain gauge

NOTIONS
Yarn Needle
Stitch Markers, 1 locking, 2 ring makers

GAUGE
23 sts and 48 rows = 4" in Garter st, unblocked
23 sts and 36 rows = 4" in Garter st, blocked

For pattern support, contact
amidwintersknit@gmail.com

Notes:
Bright stripes of beautiful color zing through the fun and unusual shape of this long triangular shawl. Garter ridges, yarn overs, and simple decreases combine with a 22-ridge stripe design to create the illusion of luminous zig-zags.

The Eclectic Electric Shawl is a long, arrow-shaped shawl, worked flat from the point to the short side. The colors repeat in different stripe configurations 4 times, ending with a border.

M1: Make one st by lifting the P bump from previous row onto left needle and K 1 st into it.
Sk2p: Sl1, K2tog, PSSO; 2 st dec

Stitch Pattern (worked flat)
The pattern is worked in Garter st, with four different Shaping Rows worked on the RS. All WS rows are knit across in the same color as the previous RS row. Refer to the chart for which Shaping Row to use for each RS row.

Shaping Row 1 (R1): K to M, SM, YO, K to M, YO, SM, K to end. 2 sts inc.
Shaping Row 2 (R2): K to M, SM, YO, K to 1 st before center stitch, Sk2p, K to M, YO, SM, K to end.
Shaping Row 3 (R3): K1, M1, K to M, SM, YO, K to 1 st before center stitch, Sk2p, K to M, YO, SM, K to last stitch, M1, K1. 2 sts inc.
Shaping Row 4 (R4): K1, M1, K to M, SM, YO, K to M, YO, SM, K to last stitch, M1, K1. 4 sts inc.

Reading the Charts
Charts are read from the bottom. R1, R2, etc. indicates which Shaping Row to use on that row. White squares represent rows worked in MC while grey squares represent C1, C2, and C3 color rows. Each chart is worked 3 times, once for each color. Knit chart with grey squares as C1, after finishing chart, restart with grey squares as C2, finish chart, then restart again with grey squares as C3, finish chart and move on to next section.

Changing Colors
Colors can be carried up the side of work where changes occur every other ridge. However, with all other color change sections, yarn should be broken off leaving a 4-5" tail to weave in after completion and rejoined as indicated in chart.

DIRECTIONS

Section A
With C1 CO 7sts.

Set-up Row (WS): K3, PM, K1, PM, K3. Mark center st on RS with a locking stitch marker on the st, not the needle. As work progresses, the center st marker will need to be moved up every few rows.

Work Chart A with MC and C1. 33 sts.

Notes:
For C1 ONLY, use R1 for the second row. All other color repeats, use R2 as shown.

Work Chart A with MC and C2. 57 sts.
Work Chart A with MC and C3. 81 sts.

Section B
Work Chart B with MC and C1. 99 sts.
Work Chart B with MC and C2. 117 sts.
Work Chart B with MC and C3. 135 sts.

Section C
Work Chart C with MC and C1. 159 sts.
Work Chart C with MC and C2. 183 sts.
Work Chart C with MC and C3. 207 sts.

Section D
Work Chart D with MC and C1. 221 sts.
Work Chart D with MC and C2. 235 sts.
Work Chart D with MC and C3. 249 sts.

Final Border
With MC, work R1 once and R2 3 times. 251 sts.
BO very loosely.

Finishing
Weave in ends, block to diagram.
Note on blocking: This shawl has an enormous amount of stretch as it is knit on the bias. Pre-blocking measurement of the center spine will be approximately 45in.

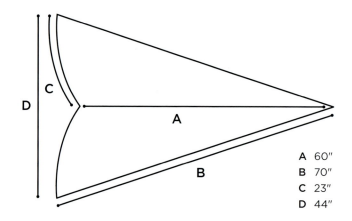

A 60"
B 70"
C 23"
D 44"

Chart A

	1
R3	22
R1	21
R2	20
R1	19
R2	18
R1	17 ■
R2	16
R1	15 ■
R2	14
R1	13 ■
R2	12
R1	11
R2	10
R1	9 ■
R2	8
R1	7 ■
R2	6
R1	5
R2	4 ■
R1	3
*R2	2 ■
R1	1 ■

Chart B

	1
R4	22
R2	21
R2	20
R1	19 ■
R2	18 ■
R2	17 ■
R1	16 ■
R2	15
R2	14
R1	13 ■
R2	12
R2	11 ■
R1	10
R2	9
R2	8 ■
R1	7
R2	6
R2	5
R1	4
R2	3
R2	2
R1	1 ■

Chart C

	1
R3	22
R1	21 ■
R2	20
R1	19
R2	18
R1	17
R2	16
R1	15
R2	14
R1	13
R2	12
R1	11 ■
R2	10
R1	9
R2	8
R1	7
R2	6
R1	5
R2	4
R1	3 ■
R2	2
R1	1 ■

Chart D

	1
R3	22 ■
R1	21 ■
R2	20 ■
R2	19 ■
R2	18 ■
R1	17 ■
R2	16 ■
R2	15
R2	14 ■
R1	13
R2	12
R2	11 ■
R2	10 ■
R1	9 ■
R2	8 ■
R2	7 ■
R2	6 ■
R1	5
R2	4 ■
R2	3
R2	2
R1	1

Legend

- ■ C1, C2, or C3
- R1 Shaping Row 1
- R2 Shaping Row 2
- R3 Shaping Row 3
- R4 Shaping Row 4

Note:
R1-R4 indicates which Shaping Row to use on the row. White squares represent rows worked in MC while grey squares represent a contrast color row. Each chart is worked three times, once for each color.

*For C1 ONLY, use R1 for the second row. All other color repeats, use R2 as shown.

FLUSH SHAWL

by Courtney Spainhower

FINISHED MEASUREMENTS
52.5" wide, 26.25" deep

YARN
Knit Picks Hawthorne Speckle Hand Paint (80% Superwash Fine Highland Wool, 20% Polyamide (Nylon); 357 yards/100g): MC Sherbet Speckle 27217, 1 skein

Knit Picks Hawthorne Fingering Multi (80% Superwash Fine Highland Wool, 20% Polyamide; 357 yards/100g): C1 Arleta 27413, C2 Irvington 26439, 1 skein each

NEEDLES
US 6 (4mm) straight or 32" or longer circular needles, or size to obtain gauge

NOTIONS
Yarn Needle

GAUGE
32 sts and 24 rows = 4" St st, blocked

For pattern support, contact cspainhower@gmail.com

Flush Shawl

Notes:
Inspired by the warm, tingling, flushing of cheeks, color moves from one to the next using simple texture and rippled stitches. The Flush Shawl is a delicate semi-circle shawl worked from the top down, increased using simple yarn overs in Pi shaping groups.

The shawl is worked from the top down, starting with a tab and continued from the center out using Pi shaping.

Garter Stitch Pattern
Row 1 (WS): K1, P2, K to last 3 sts, P2, K1.
Row 2 (RS): K.
Rep Rows 1 and 2 for patt.

Ridge Fan Lace
(worked over multiples of 11 plus 8 sts)
Row 1: K4, *(P2tog) twice, (YO, K1) 3 times, YO, (P2tog) twice; rep from * to last 4 sts, K4.
Row 2: K1, P2, K1, P to last 4 sts, K1, P2, K1.
Row 3: K.
Row 4: Rep Row 2.
Rep Rows 1-4 for patt.

Ridge Fan Edging
(worked over multiples of 11 plus 6 sts)
Row 1: K3, *(P2tog) twice, (YO, K1) 3 times, YO, (P2tog) twice; rep from * to last 4 sts, K3.
Row 2: K1, P2, K1, P to last 4 sts, K1, P2, K1.
Row 3: K.
Row 4: **Rep Row 2.**
Rep Rows 1-4 for patt

Frilled Standard Bind-off
K1, *K next stitch leaving it on the LH needle, pass first stitch over second stitch on RH needle, K into the stitch still on the LH needle removing from LH needle, pass first stitch over second stitch on right needle; rep from * to end. Break yarn and pull tail through last stitch, pulling tight to secure.

DIRECTIONS

Tab
Using MC, loosely CO 4 sts.
Row 1 (WS): K1, P2, K1.
Row 2 (RS): Knit.
Rep Rows 1-2 5 more times, rotate work 90 degrees, PU & K 5 sts along tab edge, rotate work 90 degrees, PU & Kt 4 sts along cast-on edge. 13 sts.

Body
Row 1 (WS): K1, P2, K to last 3 sts, P2, K1.
Inc Row (RS): K4, (YO, K1) to last 4 sts, YO, K4. 19 sts.
Row 3: Rep Row 1.
Row 4: K.
Row 5: Rep Row 1.
Row 6: Rep Inc Row. 31 sts.
Rows 7-13: Work Garter Stitch Pattern.
Row 14: Rep Inc Row. 55 sts.
Rows 15-27: Work Garter Stitch Pattern.
Row 28: Rep Inc Row. 103 sts.
Row 29: K1, P2, K1, P to last 4 sts, K1, P2, K1.
Row 30: K.
Row 31: Rep Row 29.
Row 32: K4, *(K1, YO, K1) into next st, Sl1 P-wise WYIB; rep from * to last 5 sts, (K1, YO, K1) into next st, K4.
Row 33: K1, P2, K1, (K3tog TBL, Sl1 P-wise WYIB) to last 7 sts, K3tog TBL, K1, P2, K1.
Row 34: K.
Row 35: Rep Row 29.
Row 36: K3, (K1, YO, K1) into next st, K to last 4 sts, (K1, YO, K1) into next st, K3. 107 sts.
Row 37: Rep Row 29.

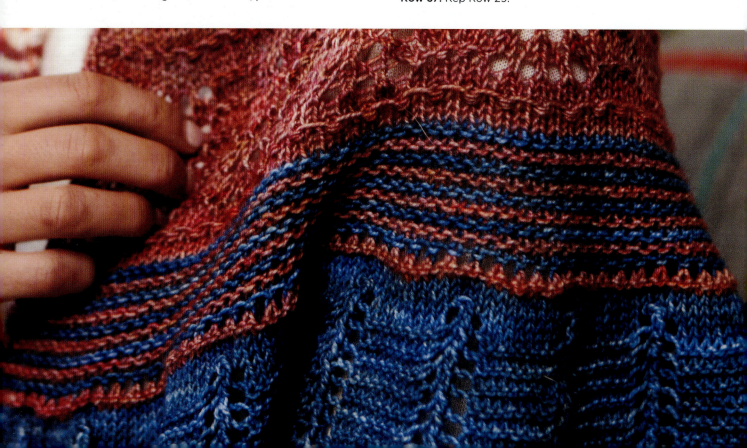

Ridge Fan Lace Section 1
Rows 38-49: Work Ridge Fan Lace, repeating Rows 1-4 three times.

Striped Garter Section
Rows 50-53: Rep Rows 32-35.
Rows 54-55: Using C1, work Garter Stitch Pattern.
Rows 56-57: Using MC, work Garter Stitch Pattern.
Row 58: Using C1, rep Inc Row. 207 sts.
Row 59: Work Row 2 of Garter Stitch Pattern.
Rows 60-61: Rep Rows 56-57.
Rows 62-63: Rep Rows 54-55.
Rows 64-67: Rep Rows 60-63.
Rows 68-69: Rep Rows 56-57.
Break MC.

Rows 70 and 72: K.
Rows 71 and 73: K1, P2, K1, P to last 4 sts, K1, P2, K1.
Rows 74-77: Rep Rows 32-35.
Row 78: K4, K2tog, K to end. 206 sts.
Row 79: K1, P2, K1, P to last 4 sts, K1, P2, K1.

Ridge Fan Lace Section 2
Rows 80-95: Work Ridge Fan Lace, repeating Rows 1-4 four times.

Row 96: K4, *(K1, YO, K1) into next st, Sl1 P-wise WYIB; rep from * to last 4 sts, K4.
Row 97: K1, P1, K1, (Sl1 P-wise WYIB, K3tog TBL) to last 4 sts.
Row 98: K4, KFB, K to end. 207 sts
Row 99: K1, P2, K1, P to last 4 sts, K1, P2, K1.

Striped Garter Section
Rows 100-101: Using C2, work Garter Stitch in pattern.
Rows 102-103: Using C1, work Garter Stitch in pattern.
Rows 104-115: Rep Rows 100-103 three times.
Rows 116-117: Rep Rows 100-101.
Row 118: Using C1 K7, (YO, K1) to last 6 sts, YO, K6. 402 sts.
Row 119: Work Row 2 of Garter Stitch Pattern.
Break C1.

Garter Columns Section
Row 120: K.
Row 121: K1, P2, K1, P to last 4 sts, K1, P2, K1.Rows 122-123: Rep Rows 120-121.
Row 124: K7, YO, *Sl2, K1, P2SSO, YO, K8, YO; rep from * to last 10 sts, Sl2, K1, P2SSO, YO, K7.
Row 125: K1, P2, K5, *P1, K10; rep from * to last 9 sts, P1, K5, P2, K1.
Rows 126-147: Rep Rows 124-125 11 more times.
Row 148: K.
Row 149: K1, P2, K1, P to last 4 sts, K1, P2, K1.

Ridge Fan Edging Section
Rows 150-154: Work Ridge Fan Edging, repeating Rows 1-4 once, then Rep row 1 once more.
On WS row, BO using the Frilled Standard Bind-Off method.

Finishing
Weave in ends, wash and block to measurements.

FRACTAL SHAWL

by Cheryl Toy

FINISHED MEASUREMENTS
66" semi-circular wingspan, 30" deep at deepest point

YARN
Knit Picks Preciosa Tonal Fingering (100% Merino Wool; 437 yards/100g): MC Blue Skies 26942; C1 Crest 26947, 2 skeins each

NEEDLES
US 5 (3.75mm) circular needles, 40" or size to obtain gauge

NOTIONS
Stitch Markers (optional)

GAUGE
18 sts and 34 rows = 4" in St st, blocked

For pattern support, contact cheryl@littlechurchknits.com

Notes:
Fractures in stone, dislocation and shifting plates inspire the Fractal Shawl with directional stitch movement echoing fault lines and the subtle displacement of rock under pressure.

The Fractal Shawl is a generously sized semi-circular wrap worked from the center of the upper edge outward. A classic ripple pattern is re-imagined in this semi-circular shawl, using three interpretations of the original stitch pattern to create a fabric that moves from a chevron styled solid to the openness of Arrowhead Lace. Directional increases are used to create a flared edge that is three dimensional in fullness.

Make 1 Left-leaning Stitch (M1L)
With left needle tip, lift strand between needles from front to back. Knit the lifted loop through the back.

Make 1 Right-leaning Stitch (M1R)
With left needle tip, lift strand between needles from back to front. Knit the lifted loop through the front.

Centered Double Decrease (CDD)
Sl1 K-wise, K2tog, PSSO.

Picot Bind-Off
*Using the knitted method, CO 2 sts. BO 6 sts, placing remaining st back onto left needle; rep from * until all sts have been bound off.

When using the charts, read the chart RS rows (odd numbers) from right to left, and WS rows (even numbers) from left to right. Chart B has been broken up into 3 charts: Right, Center Repeat, and Left. For each row, you will work the Right chart, work the Center Repeat, repeating this chart across the row, then work the Left chart. Optional stitch markers may be used to mark pattern repeats.

DIRECTIONS

Shawl Set Up
With MC, CO 5 sts.
Row 1 (RS): K2, YO, K1, YO, K2. 7 sts.
Row 2: K2, P to last 2 sts, K2.
Row 3: K2, YO twice, K1, YO, K to last 3 sts, YO, K1, YO twice, K2. 13 sts.
Row 4: K2, P1, P1 TBL, P to double YO, P1 TBL, P1, K2.
Rep Rows 3 and 4 once more. 19 sts.

Shawl Body
Chevron Section
Row 1 (RS): K2, YO twice, K1, YO, K1, *M1L, K4, CDD, K4, M1R, K1; rep from * to last 3 sts, YO, K1, YO twice, K2. 6 sts inc.
Row 2, 4, 6 and 8: K2, P1, P1 TBL, P to double YO, P1 TBL, P1, K2.
Row 3: K2, YO twice, K1, YO, K4, *M1L, K4, CDD, K4, M1R, K1; rep from * to last 6 sts, K3, YO, K1, YO twice, K2. 6 sts inc.
Row 5: K2, YO twice, K1, YO, K7, *M1L, K4, CDD, K4, M1R, K1; rep from * to last 9 sts, K6, YO, K1, YO twice, K2. 6 sts inc.
Row 7: K2, YO twice, K1, YO, K10, *M1L, K4, CDD, K4, M1R, K1; rep from * to last 12 sts, K9, YO, K1, YO twice, K2. 6 sts inc.
Work Rows 1 - 8 eleven times total, then Rows 1 and 2 once more. (289 sts)

Eyelet Chevron SectionC
Work Rows 1-12 of Chart A twice. 337 sts.

Eyelet Increase Section
Work Rows 1-38 of Chart B once. 705 sts.

Arrowhead Lace Border
Switch to C1 and work Rows 39-40 of Chart B, rep until border measures 8" in depth.
BO using Picot Bind-off.

Finishing
Weave in ends, wash and block to diagram.

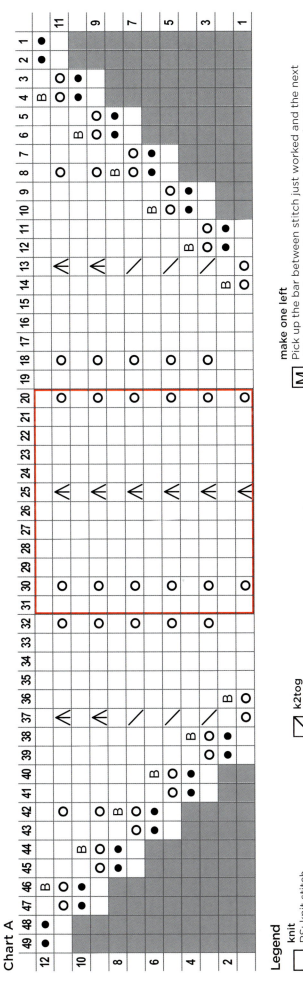

Chart B (Left)

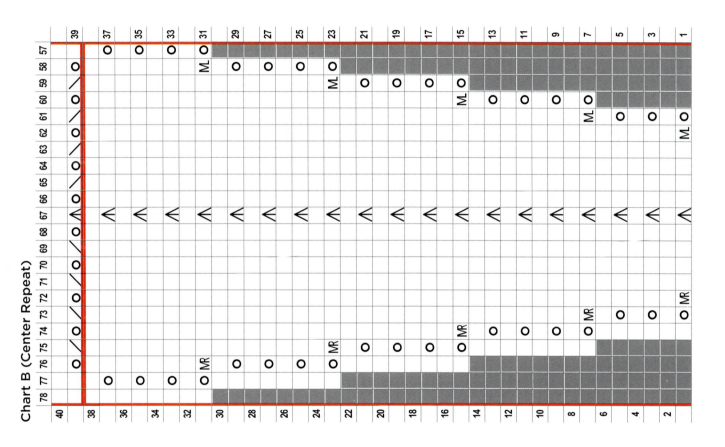

Chart B (Center Repeat)

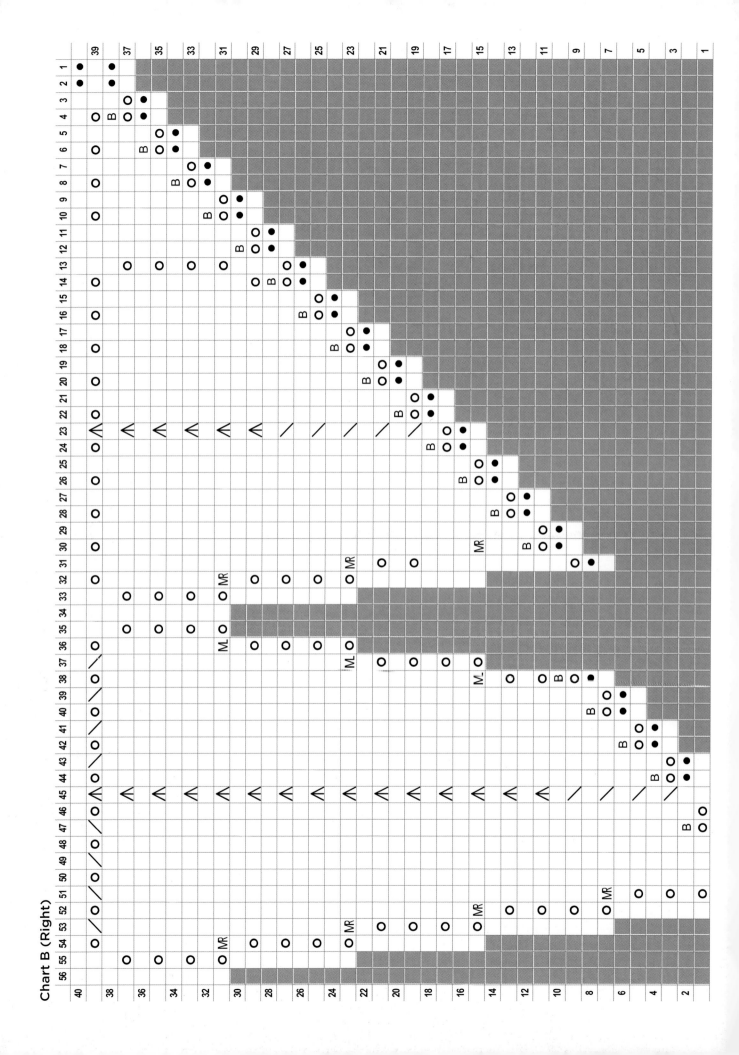

Chart B (Right)

ILANA WRAP
by Katrine Birkenwasser

FINISHED MEASUREMENTS
13" x 73"

YARN
Knit Picks Hawthorne Speckle Hand Paint (80% Superwash Fine Highland Wool, 20% Polyamide (Nylon); 357 yards/100g): MC City Lights Speckle 27220, 3 skeins

Knit Picks Hawthorne Kettle Dye (80% Superwash Fine Highland Wool, 20% Polyamide (Nylon); 357 yards/100g): C1 Blackbird 26698, C2 Slate 26688, 1 skein each

NEEDLES
US 5 (3.75mm) straight or circular needles, or size to obtain gauge

NOTIONS
Yarn Needle
Stitch Markers

GAUGE
22 sts and 43 rows = 4" in garter stitch, blocked
Gauge for this project is not important, but it will affect the size of the finished object and amount of yarn needed.

For pattern support, contact
birkenwasseranhohe@gmail.com

Notes:
Ilana Wrap is the perfect accessory for showing off beautiful speckled colorways. Contrast colors on the sides take a bit of the fuzz off and give it a sharp look. It's easy to wear by wrapping it around your neck for warmth and added detail to your outfit. There's enough length to wrap it around your shoulders when it gets chilly in the evening.

The wrap is worked flat in garter stitch. The rhomboid shape is created with simple increases on one end and decreases on the other end. Simple intarsia on the sides turns into triangles as the shape of the wrap forms.

Garter Stitch (worked flat over any number of sts)
All Rows: K to end.

DIRECTIONS

Throughout the pattern, one st is dec at the beginning and one st inc at the end of all even rows. Therefore, the number of sts stays the same.

Using C1, CO 102 sts.
Row 1 (WS): K to end.
Row 2 (RS): K1, K2TOG, K to last 2 sts, KFB, K1.
Rows 3-6: Rep Rows 1-2 twice.
Row 7: K to end.

Triangles
Row 8 (RS): K1, K2TOG, K23, PM, switch to MC, K74, PM, switch to C2, KFB, K1.
Row 9 (WS): K to M, SM, switch to MC, K to M, SM, switch to C1, K remaining sts.
Row 10: K1, K2TOG, K to M, SM, switch to MC, K to M, SM, switch to C2, K to last 2 sts, KFB, K1.
Rows 11-52: Rep Rows 9-10 21 more times (3 sts in C1, 74 in MC, and 25 in C2).
Row 53: Rep Row 9.

Rep the Triangles pattern (Rows 8-53) 11 more times or until desired length. When transitioning from Row 53 to Row 8, carry MC yarn by wrapping it around C1 every 5 sts to avoid long floats on WS. Work similarly with C2 at the end of the row.

Finish with C2. Break all yarns.
With C2, rep Rows 2-7.
BO all sts.

Finishing
Weave in ends, wash and block to diagram. Make sure that the triangles are right-angled!

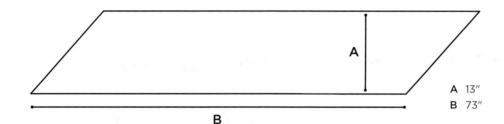

A 13"
B 73"

IRIS SHAWL

by Violet LeBeaux

FINISHED MEASUREMENTS
Finished Measurements
56" (74") wide x 14" (18") length from center to edge of curve
Note that as the shawl is mostly garter stitch, it is very stretchy until the I-Cord is added to stabilize the edge

YARN
Knit Picks Bare Gloss Fingering
(70% Merino Wool, 30% Silk; 440 yards/100g): MC Bare 23998, 1 skein
Knit Picks Gloss Fingering
(70% Merino Wool, 30% Silk; 220 yards/50g): C1 Robot 25015, 1; C2 Cranberry 25378, 1 ball each

NEEDLES
US 6 (4mm) straight or circular needles, or size to obtain gauge
US 7 (4.5mm) DPN or circular needles, or size needed for for I-Cord edging

NOTIONS
Yarn Needle

GAUGE
18 sts and 40 rows = 4" in Garter st, blocked

For pattern support, contact
violetlebeaux@gmail.com

Notes:
Iris is a crescent shaped garter stitch shawl, and features alternating complimentary-colored stripes, an eyelet section for texture and a contrasting applied I-Cord edging to tie it all together. It is worked flat from the center out and with the majority of the shawl in garter stitch, this a great project for beginners.

I-Cord and Applied I-Cord Edging
I-Cord is a thin tube of knitting which is only a few stitches wide. It is knit in the round using either DPN or circular needles. The look is achieved by casting on a few stitches, knitting them then moving them back to the left needle to start the next row. Applied I-Cord edging is the same principle but with an additional stitch picked up from the edge of your main work every row to attach it on.
There are some great tips in this article including using it as a bind off if you are unfamiliar with the process: http://tutorials.knitpicks.com/i-cord-bind-off/.

DIRECTIONS

Shawl
The shawl is worked flat starting from the top center.

Stripes
With MC loosely CO 8 sts.
Rows 1-2: With MC K1, M1, K until last st, M1, K1.
Row 3-4: With C1 K1, M1, K until last st, M1, K1.
Repeat Rows 1-4 another 25 (35) times or until the work reaches 10.75 (14.75)" in length, then repeat Rows 1-2 once more.
Break C1 yarn and secure end.

Contrasting Section
Rows 1-2: With C2 K1, M1, K until last st, M1, K1.
Row 3: With MC, K1, M1, K until last st, M1, K1.
Row 4: K1, M1, *P2tog, YO; rep from * until last st, M1, K1.
Repeat Rows 1-4 twice more, then repeat Rows 1-2 once more. BO all sts.
Wash and block to diagram before moving on to the Applied I-Cord Edging.

Applied I-Cord Edging
An I-Cord edge is worked using C2 around the entire shawl. With the right side facing, start the edging from a corner and work down the straight edge.
With C2 CO 3 sts to right needle.
Set Up Rnd: PU and K 1 st from edge of work onto left needle. Sl 3 sts from RH needle back to LH needle.
Rnd 1: K2, Sl1, K1, PSSO, PU and K 1 st from edge of work, Sl 3 sts from RH needle back to LH needle.
Repeat Rnd 1 until you have made it the entire way around the edge of the shawl.
When turning a corner, complete Rnd 1 twice in the corner stitch to provide enough I-Cord to create a crisp pointed corner. Make sure to watch your tension when working on the curved edge because if your I-Cord is too tight it will affect the final shape of the shawl. If you find that the shape is being warped, step up a needle size.
Once you have made your way fully around the shawl, BO all sts and graft the end to the start edge.

Finishing
Weave in ends, wash and re-block if needed.

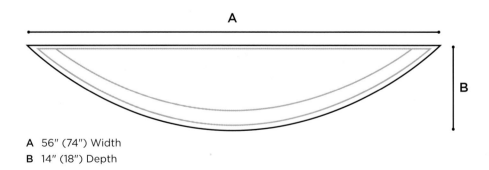

A 56" (74") Width
B 14" (18") Depth

JOYCEJUBILAIR

by Renate Kamm

FINISHED MEASUREMENTS
60" wide at top edge, 90" wide at the bottom lace edge, 12.25" deep

YARN
Knit Picks Stroll Hand Painted
(75% Superwash Merino Wool, 25% Nylon; 462 yards/100g); MC Northern Lights 26733, 1 skein
Knit Picks Stroll Sock
(75% Superwash Merino Wool, 25% Nylon; 231 yards/50g); C1 Sapphire Heather 24590, 2 balls

NEEDLES
US 3 (3.25mm) 47" or longer circular needle, or size to obtain gauge
Exact gauge is not necessary, but may affect the amount of yarn needed

NOTIONS
Yarn Needle
Removable Stitch Marker
396 Beads size 8 and steel crochet hook size 14 to mount the beads (Optional)

GAUGE
24 sts and 48 rows = 4" in Garter Stitch, blocked

For pattern support, contact
oberpfalzerin@hotmail.com

Notes:

The Joycejubilaire shawl was created to embody strength and stability as a gift for a very ill friend. With its arches and emphasized columns design the shawl mirrors the architectural strength of bridges, or the mighty strength of arched walkways with their supporting columns. The shawl begins with a basic garter stitch crescent body that is framed both on top and bottom edges by small lace border arches. Then the main bright colored lace is added, then finished with larger, optionally beaded, arches and a small eyelet strip. The shawl only looks complicated, but the lace is not difficult at all. The pattern is detailed with row-by-row instructions and also charted.

If working from the charts, read the charts RS rows from right to left, and WS rows from left to right.

Slip With Yarn in Front (SL WYIF)
Slip stitch as if to purl, holding working yarn to front. Work the same for both RS and WS rows.

Crescent Body Pattern A
Setup Row (WS): K.
Row 1 (RS): (K1, YO) 4 times, K1.
Row 2 and all even numbered rows: K.
Row 3: (K1, YO) twice, K to last 2 sts, (YO, K1) twice.
Rep Rows 2-3 for pattern.

Border Lace Pattern B
Setup Row (WS): With MC, K4, P2, K to last 6 sts, P2, K2, Sl2 P-wise WYIF.
Row 1 (RS): K2, P2, K2, *P1, (P2tog, YO) 4 times, P1, (YO, P2tog) 4 times; rep from * to last 7 sts, P1, K2, P2, Sl2 P-wise WYIF.
Row 2: K4, P2, K to last 6 sts, P2, K2, Sl2 P-wise WYIF.
Row 3: With C1, K2, P2, K2, *P1, K8; rep from * to last 7 sts, P1, K2, P2, Sl2 P-wise WYIF.
Row 4: K4, P2, K1, *P8, K1; rep from * to last 6 sts, P2, K2, Sl2 P-wise WYIF.
Row 5: K2, P2, K2, *P1, K2tog 3 times, (YO, K1) twice, YO, P1, (YO, K1) twice, YO, SSK 3 times; rep from * to last 7 sts, P1, K2, P2, Sl2 P-wise WYIF.
Row 6: Rep Row 4.
Row 7: With MC, rep Row 3.
Row 8: Rep Row 2.
Row 9: Rep Row 1.
Row 10: Rep Row 2.

Transition Lace Pattern C
Setup Row (WS): With MC, K to last 2 sts, Sl2 P-wise WYIF.
Row 1 (RS): K2, *P1, (P2tog, YO) 4 times, P1, (YO, P2tog) 4 times; rep from * to last 3 sts, P1, Sl2 P-wise WYIF.
Row 2: K last 2 sts, Sl2 P-wise WYIF.
Row 3: With C1, K2, *P1, K8; rep from * to last 3 sts, P1, Sl2 P-wise WYIF.
Row 4: K3, *P8, K1; rep from * to last 2 sts, Sl2 P-wise WYIF.
Row 5: K2, *P1, K2tog 3 times, (YO, K1) twice, YO, P1, (YO, K1) twice, YO, SSK 3 times; rep from * to last 3 sts, P1, Sl2 P-wise WYIF.
Row 6: Rep Row 4.
Row 7: With MC, rep Row 3.
Row 8: Rep Row 2.
Row 9: Rep Row 1.
Row 10: Rep Row 2.

Main Lace Pattern D
Row 1 (RS): With C1, K2, *P1, K2tog 3 times, (YO, K1) 5 times, YO, SSK 3 times; rep from * to last 3 sts, P1, Sl2 P-wise WYIF.
Row 2 (WS): K3, *P6, (P1 TBL, K1) twice, P1 TBL, P6, K1; rep from * to last 2 sts, Sl2 P-wise WYIF.
Row 3: K2, *P1, K3, K2tog, YO, (P1, K1 TBL) 3 times, P1, YO, SSK, K3; rep from * to last 3 sts, P1, Sl2 P-wise WYIF.
Row 4: K3, *P5, (K1, P1 TBL) 3 times, K1, P5, K1; rep from * to last 2 sts, Sl2 P-wise WYIF.
Row 5: K2, *P1, K2, K2tog, YO, (K1 TBL, P1) 4 times, K1 TBL, YO, SSK, K2; rep from * to last 3 sts, P1, Sl2 P-wise WYIF.
Row 6: K3, *P3, (K1, P1 TBL) 5 times, K1, P3, K1; rep from * to last 2 sts, Sl2 P-wise WYIF.
Row 7: K2, *P1, K1, K2tog, YO, (P1, K1 TBL) 5 times, P1, YO, SSK, K1; rep from * to last 3 sts, P1, Sl2 P-wise WYIF.
Row 8: Rep Row 6.
Row 9: K2, *P1, K2tog, YO, (K1 TBL, P1) 6 times, K1 TBL, YO, SSK; rep from * to last 3 sts, P1, Sl2 P-wise WYIF.
Row 10: K3, *P2, (P1 TBL, K1) 6 times, P1 TBL, P2, K1; rep from * to last 2 sts, Sl2 P-wise WYIF.
Row 11: K2, *P1, SSK 3 times, (YO, K1) 5 times, YO, K2tog 3 times; rep from * to last 3 sts, P1, Sl2 P-wise WYIF.
Row 12: K3, *P17, K1; rep from * to last 2 sts, Sl2 P-wise WYIF.
Row 13: Rep Row 11.
Row 14: Rep Row 12.
Row 15: Rep Row 11.
Row 16: Rep Row 12.
Row 17: Rep Row 1.
Row 18: Rep Row 2.
Row 19: Rep Row 3.
Row 20: K3, *P5, K1, P1 TBL, K1, YO, P1 TBL, YO, K1, P1 TBL, K1, P5, K1; rep from * to last 2 sts, Sl2 P-wise WYIF.
Row 21: K2, *P1, K2, K2tog, YO, K1 TBL, P1, (K1 TBL, P2) twice, K1 TBL, P1, K1 TBL, YO, SSK, K2, rep from * to last 3 sts, P1, Sl2 P-wise WYIF.
Row 22: K3 *P3, (K1, P1 TBL) twice, (K2, P1 TBL) twice, K1, P1 TBL, K1, P3, K1; rep from * to last 2 sts, Sl2 P-wise WYIF.
Row 23: K2, *P1, K1, K2tog, YO, (P1, K1 TBL) twice, (P2, K1 TBL) twice, P1, K1 TBL, P1, YO, SSK, K1; rep from * to last 3 sts, P1, Sl2 P-wise WYIF.
Row 24: Rep Row 22.
Row 25: K2, *P1, K2tog, YO, (K1 TBL, P1) 3 times, YO, P1, K1 TBL, P1, YO, (P1, K1 TBL) 3 times, YO, SSK; rep from * to last 3 sts, P1, Sl2 P-wise WYIF.
Row 26: K3, *P2, (P1 TBL, K1) 8 times, P1 TBL, P2, K1; rep from * to lasts 2 sts, Sl2 P-wise WYIF.
Row 27: K2, *P1, SSK 3 times, (YO, K1) 3 times, YO, CDD, YO, (K1, YO) 3 times, K2tog 3 times; rep from * to last 3 sts, P1, Sl2 P-wise WYIF.
Row 28: K3, *P21, K1; rep from * to last 2 sts, Sl2 P-wise WYIF.
Row 29: K2, *P1, SSK 2 times, K2, (YO, K1) 3 times, YO, CDD, YO, (K1, YO) 3 times, K2, K2tog 2 times; rep from * to last 3 sts, P1, Sl2 P-wise WYIF.

Row 30: K3, *P23, K1; rep from * to last 2 sts, Sl2 P-wise WYIF.
Row 31: K2, *P1, SSK 2 times, YO, CDD, YO, (K1, YO) 3 times, CDD, YO, (K1, YO) 3 times, CDD, YO, K2tog 2 times; rep from * to last 3 sts, P1, Sl2 P-wise WYIF.
Row 32: Rep Row 30.
Row 33: K2, *P1, K2, (YO, CDD, YO, K1) 5 times, K1; rep from * to last 3 sts, P1, Sl2 P-wise WYIF.
Row 34: Rep Row 30.
Row 35: With MC, K2, *P1, K23; rep from * to last 3 sts, P1, Sl2 P-wise WYIF.
Row 36: K last 2 sts, Sl2 P-wise WYIF.
Row 37: K2, *P1, (P2tog, YO) 11 times, P1; rep from * to last 3 sts, P1, Sl2 P-wise WYIF.
Row 38: Rep Row 36.

Jeny's Surprisingly Stretchy Bind-off
Processing a K st: Wrap the yarn around the RH needle in a reverse yarn over, from back to front. K 1 st. Pull the YO over the K st.
Processing a P st: Wrap the yarn around the RH needle in a yarn over, from front to back. P 1 st. Pull the YO over the P st.
BO Step 1: Work first st as described above; 1 st on the RH needle.
BO Step 2: Process the next st correctly, i.e. working the YO the way described above and K or P as needed.
BO Step 3: Pull the 1st st on your RH needle over the 2nd st on your RH needle and off the needle.
Repeat Steps 2 and 3 until 1 st remains. Cut the yarn and pull it through the last st.

DIRECTIONS

Main Shawl Body
With MC loosely CO 5 sts.
Setup Row (WS): K.
Work Crescent Body Pattern A for 73 Rows, ending with a RS row. 153 sts.
Place a removable marker at the start of an odd numbered row to mark the RS of the shawl fabric.

Right Crescent Arm
Continue incs on the crescent outside edge while working the short rows to create the right crescent arm.
Row 74 (WS): K60, PM, K33, PM, K to end.
Row 75 (RS): K1, YO, K1, YO, K to the 1st M, turn.
Row 76: Sl1, K to end.
Row 77: K1, YO, K1, YO, K to 3 sts before the 1st M, turn.
Row 78: Sl1, K to end.
Row 79: K1, YO, K1, YO, K to 3 sts before the previous short row turn, turn.

Continue as established, knitting 3 less sts on the inside edge and increasing 2 sts on the outside edge until there are 170 sts to the right of the center 33sts, ending with a WS row. 263 sts.

Next Row (RS): K to M, SM, K to M, SM, K to last 2 sts, YO, K1, YO, K1.

Left Crescent Arm
Create the left arm of the crescent shape, continuing the incs on the crescent outside edge.
Next Row (WS): K to the 1st M, turn.
Next Row (RS): Sl1, K to last 2 sts, YO, K1, YO, K1.
Next Row: K to 3 sts before M, turn.

Continue to increase 2 sts on the crescent outside edge while knitting 3 less sts on the inside edge until there are 170 sts to the left of the middle 33 sts, ending with a RS row. 373 sts.

Border Lace Pattern
Work Border Lace Pattern B, repeating the pattern repeat 20 times across.
BO all sts firmly using a Knitted BO.

Picking Up Sts for Edging

Turn the crescent shape upside down and with RS facing, attach the MC at the right edge, before the first hole created by the YOs. Pull the yarn through the first st. Create another st by pulling yarn through the YO hole and add a YO, *pull a st through the next hole along the edge, add a YO; rep from * to end, pull st through last st on edge. 379 sts.

Transition Lace Pattern

Setup Row (WS): K100, (KFB, K7) 11 times, K1, (K7, KFB) 11 times, K to last 2 sts, Sl2 P-wise WYIF.

Work Rows 1-10 of Transition Lace Pattern C, changing to C1 at Row 3 and back to MC at Row 7.

Main Lace Pattern

With C1 work Rows 1-34 of Main Lace Pattern D. Switch to MC and work Rows 35-38 of Main Lace Pattern D. BO at the next RS row using Jeny's Surprisingly Stretchy BO.

Finishing

Weave in ends, wet block to diagram.

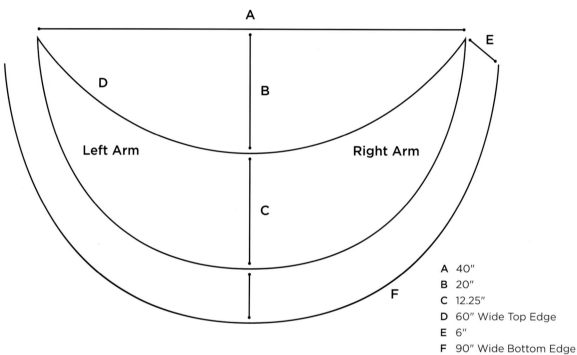

Note: The arches add 1" to the length of the shawl to 13.25"

- A 40"
- B 20"
- C 12.25"
- D 60" Wide Top Edge
- E 6"
- F 90" Wide Bottom Edge

Legend

knit
RS: knit stitch
WS: purl stitch

purl
RS: purl stitch
WS: knit stitch

yo
Yarn Over

knit tbl
RS: Knit stitch through back loop
WS: Purl stitch through back loop

k2tog
Knit two stitches together as one stitch

p2tog
Purl two stitches together.

ssk
Slip one stitch as if to knit. Slip another stitch as if to knit. Insert left-hand needle into front of these two stitches and knit them together.

slip wyif
RS and WS: Slip stitch as if to purl, with yarn in front.

Central Double Dec
Slip first and second stitches together as if to knit. Knit one stitch. Pass two slipped stitches over the knit stitch.

MC

C1

Place Bead (optional)

No Stitch

Pattern Repeat

Crescent Body Pattern A

Border Lace Pattern B

Transition Lace Pattern C

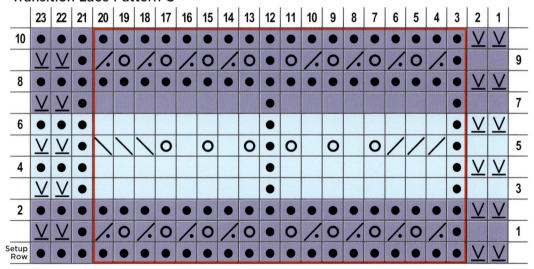

Main Lace Pattern D

JUNCTION SHAWL

by Tetiana Otruta

FINISHED MEASUREMENTS
80" wingspan, 20" deep, relaxed after blocking.

YARN
Knit Picks Hawthorne Speckle Hand Paint (80% Superwash Fine Highland Wool, 20% Polyamide (Nylon); 375 yards/100g): MC Cosmic Speckle 26871, 1 skein
Knit Picks Hawthorne Tonal Hand Paint (80% Superwash Fine Highland Wool, 20% Polyamide (Nylon); 375 yards/100g): C1 Klamath Falls 27404, 1 skein

NEEDLES
US 5 (3.75 mm) 32" or longer circular needle, or size to obtain gauge

NOTIONS
Stitch Markers (optional)
Yarn Needle

GAUGE
20 sts and 44 rows = 4" in Garter st, unblocked
18 sts and 36 rows = 4" in Garter st, lightly blocked

For pattern support, contact
tetianaotruta@gmail.com

Notes:
Junction Shawl is a two color asymmetric triangular shawl worked sideways in garter stitch with eyelets and simple textured lace.

If using Chart A for Section 3 Lace, read RS rows from right to left and WS rows from left to right.

Cable Cast-On (for optional Picot BO): *Insert RH needle between the first two stitches on LH needle, wrap yarn around needle and bring through. Transfer the newly created stitch onto LH needle; rep from * until you have cast on the specified number of sts.

Garter Shaping Pattern
Row 1: KFB, K1, M1, K to last 2 sts, K2tog.
Row 2: K to end.
Rep Rows 1-2 for patt.

DIRECTIONS

Section 1
With MC, CO 3 sts. Work the following rows with MC if nothing stated otherwise.
Row 1 (RS): KFB, K2. 4 sts.
Row 2, 4: K to end.
Row 3: K2, M1, K2. 5 sts.

Work Rows 1-2 of Garter Shaping pattern twenty-nine times. 34 sts.
Eyelet Row (RS): KFB, K1, YO, *K2tog, YO, rep from * to last 2 sts, K2tog. 35 sts.
Next Row (WS): K to end.
Work Rows 1-2 of Garter Shaping pattern five times. 40 sts.
Work Eyelet Row and WS Row once. 41 sts.
Work Rows 1-2 of Garter Shaping pattern thirteen times. 54 sts.
With C1, work Rows 1-2 of Garter Shaping pattern once. 55 sts.
With MC, work Rows 1-2 of Garter Shaping pattern seven times. 62 sts.
Work Eyelet Row and WS Row once. 63 sts.
Work Rows 1-2 of Garter Shaping pattern six times. 69 sts.
With C1, work Rows 1-2 of Garter Shaping pattern once. 70 sts.
With MC, work Rows 1-2 of Garter Shaping pattern once. 71 sts.
With C1, work Rows 1-2 of Garter Shaping pattern once. 72 sts.
With MC, work Rows 1-2 of Garter Shaping pattern six times. 78 sts.
Work Eyelet Row and WS Row once. 79 sts.
Work Rows 1-2 of Garter Shaping pattern eleven times. 90 sts.
Work Eyelet Row and WS Row once. 91 sts.
Work Rows 1-2 of Garter Shaping pattern seven times. 98 sts.
Work Eyelet Row and WS Row once. 99 sts.
Work Rows 1-2 of Garter Shaping pattern once. 100 sts.

Section 2a
Rows 1-2: With C1, work Rows 1-2 of Garter Shaping pattern once. 101 sts.
Rows 3-4: With MC, work Rows 1-2 of Garter Shaping pattern once. 102 sts.
Row 5 (Eyelet Row): With MC, KFB, K1, YO, *K2tog, YO, rep from * to last 2 sts, K2tog. 103 sts.
Row 6: With MC, K to end.
Rows 7-8: With C1, work Rows 1-2 of Garter Shaping pattern once. 104 sts.
Rows 9-10: With MC, work Rows 1-2 of Garter Shaping pattern once. 105 sts.
Row 11 (Eyelet Row 2): With MC, KFB, K2, YO, *K2tog, YO, rep from * to last 2 sts, K2tog. 106 sts.
Row 12: With MC, K to end.

Rep Rows 1-12 one more time. 112 sts.
Rep Rows 1-6 once. 115 sts.

Rep Rows 1-4 six times. 127 sts.

Section 2b
Rows 1-2: With C1, work Rows 1-2 of Garter Shaping pattern once. 128 sts.
Row 3 (Eyelet Row): With C1, KFB, K1, YO, *K2tog, YO, rep from * to last 2 sts, K2tog. 129 sts.
Row 4: With C1, K to end.
Rows 5-6: With MC, work Rows 1-2 of Garter Shaping pattern once. 130 sts.
Rows 7-8: With C1, work Rows 1-2 of Garter Shaping pattern once. 131 sts.
Row 9 (Eyelet Row 2): With C1, KFB, K2, YO, *K2tog, YO, rep from * to last 2 sts, K2tog. 132 sts.
Row 10: With C1, K to end.
Rows 11-12: With MC, work Rows 1-2 of Garter Shaping pattern once. 133 sts.

Rep Rows 1-12 one more time. 139 sts.
Rep Rows 1-6 once. 142 sts.

Inc Row (RS): With C1, KFB, (K1, M1) twice, K to 2 sts from end, K2tog. 144 sts.
Next Row (WS): K to end.
Rep Inc Row and WS Row 2 times more. 148 sts.

Section 3, Lace
Work Section 3 Lace with C1 and using Chart A or from written instructions.

Row 1 (RS): KFB, K1, M1, K to last 2 sts, K2tog. 149 sts.
Row 2 (WS): K5, (P2, K4) rep to end.
Row 3: KFB, K1, M1, (K1, K2tog, YO2, SKP, K1) rep to last 3 sts, K2tog, K1. 150 sts.
Row 4: K2, (K1, P2, K1, P1, K1) rep to last 4 sts, K1, P1, K2.
Row 5: KFB, K1, M1, YO, SKP, (K2tog, YO, K2 TBL, YO, SKP) rep to last 2 sts, K2tog. 151 sts.
Row 6: K1, (P1, K4, P1) rep to last 6 sts, P1, K5.
Row 7: KFB, K1, M1, K1, (K1, K2tog, YO2, SKP, K1) rep to last 4 sts, K1, K2tog, K1. 152 sts.
Row 8: K3, (K1, P2, K1, P1, K1) rep to last 5 sts, K1, P1, K3.
Row 9: KFB, K1, M1, K1, YO, SKP, (K2tog, YO, K2 TBL, YO, SKP) rep to last 3 sts, K2tog, K1. 153 sts.
Row 10: K2, (P1, K4, P1) rep to last 7 sts, P1, K6.
Row 11: KFB, K1, YO, K2, (K1, K2tog, YO2, SKP, K1) rep to last 5 sts, K1, K2tog, K2. 154 sts.
Row 12: K2, P1, K1, (K1, P2, K1, P1, K1) rep to last 6 sts, K1, P1, K4.
Row 13: KFB, K1, YO, K2, YO, SKP, (K2tog, YO, K2 TBL, YO, SKP) rep to last 4 sts, K2tog, K2. 155 sts.
Row 14: K2, P1, (P1, K4, P1) rep to last 2 sts, K2.

Row 15: KFB, K1, YO2, SKP, K1, (K1, K2tog, YO2, SKP, K1) rep to last 6 sts, K1, K2tog, YO, K2tog, K1. 156 sts.

Row 16: K2, P2, K1, (K1, P2, K1, P1, K1) rep to last 7 sts, K1, P2, K1, P1, K2.

Row 17: KFB, K2, YO, K2 TBL, YO, SKP, (K2tog, YO, K2 TBL, YO, SKP) rep to last 5 sts, K2tog, YO, K2tog, K1. 157 sts.

Row 18: K2, P2, (P1, K4, P1) rep to last 3 sts, P1, K2.

Row 19: KFB, K2, YO2, SKP, K1, (K1, K2tog, YO2, SKP, K1) rep to last 7 sts, K1, K2tog, YO2, SKP, K2tog. 158 sts.

Row 20: K2, (P1, K1) twice, (K1, P2, K1, P1, K1) rep to last 2 sts, K2.

Row 21: KFB, K1, M1, (K2tog, YO, K2 TBL, YO, SKP) rep to last 6 sts, K2tog, YO, K1, K2tog, K1. 159 sts.

Row 22: K4, P1, (P1, K4, P1) rep to last 4 sts, P1, K3.

Row 23: KFB, K1, M1, K2tog, YO2, SKP, K1, (K1, K2tog, YO2, SKP, K1) rep to last 8 sts, K1, K2tog, YO2, SKP, K2tog, K1. 160 sts.

Row 24: K2, P2, K1, P1, K1, (K1, P2, K1, P1, K1) rep to last 3 sts, K3.

Row 25: KFB, K1, YO, K1, (K2tog, YO, K2 TBL, YO, SKP) rep to last 7 sts, K2tog, YO, K2, K2tog, K1. 161 sts.

Row 26: K5, P1, (P1, K4, P1) rep to last 5 sts, P1, K4.

Rep Rows 3-18 once more. 169 sts.

Chart A

Legend

knit
RS: knit stitch
WS: purl stitch

purl
RS: purl stitch
WS: knit stitch

yo
Yarn Over

knit tbl
Knit stitch through back loop.

kfb
Knit into the front and back of stitch

make one
Make one by lifting strand in between stitch just worked and next stitch. Knit into back of the thread.

k2tog
Knit two stitches together as one stitch

skp
slip one, knit one, pass slipped stitch over, knit one

No Stitch

Pattern Repeat

Section 4

With C1, work Rows 1-2 of Garter Shaping pattern three times. 172 sts.

With MC, work Rows 1-2 of Garter Shaping pattern once. 173 sts.
With C1, work Rows 1-2 of Garter Shaping pattern eight times. 181 sts.

Next row (RS): With C1, K to end. 181 sts.

Bind Off
BO on WS with C1 using Picot or Regular BO.

Picot BO
Using Cable CO, CO2 sts onto LH needle, BO 8 K-wise, *move st from RH needle to LH needle, CO2 sts onto LH needle, BO 8 K-wise, rep from * to end. Cut yarn and pull yarn tail into the last st.

Regular BO
K1, *K1, pull the first st on the RH needle over the second st and off the RH needle; rep from * to end.
Cut yarn and pull the yarn tail into the last st.

Finishing
Weave in yarn ends; trim after blocking. Soak shawl in lukewarm water (with soap for fiber if desired) for 10-15 minutes. Rinse and roll in towel to get rid of excess water. Pin out on a clean sheet or blocking board. Let dry and unpin only when dry, then trim yarn tails.

KOLOREAK

by Annika Andrea Wolke

FINISHED MEASUREMENTS
Approx. 62.5" wingspan x 31.25" deep

YARN
Knit Picks Hawthorne Speckle Hand Paint (80% Superwash Fine Highland Wool; 20% Polyamide (Nylon), 357 yards/100g): MC Blueberry Speckle 27219, 1 skein

Knit Picks Hawthorne Multi (80% Superwash Fine Highland Wool; 20% Polyamide (Nylon), 357 yards/100g): C1 Springwater 27422, 1 skein

Knit Picks Hawthorne Kettle Dye (80% Superwash Fine Highland Wool; 20% Polyamide (Nylon), 357 yards/100g): C2 Compass 26690, 2 skeins

Knit Picks Hawthorne Tonal Hand Paint (80% Superwash Fine Highland Wool; 20% Polyamide (Nylon), 357 yards/100g): C3 Klamath Falls 27404, 2 skeins

NEEDLES
US 2 (2.75mm) 60" circular needles (or 2x 32" circular needles if longer ones not available), or size to obtain gauge
US 4 (3.5mm) 60" circular needles (or 2x 32" circular needles if longer ones not available), or size to obtain gauge

NOTIONS
Yarn Needle
Stitch Markers

GAUGE
30 sts and 42 rows = 4" in St st with smaller needles, blocked
30 sts and 31 rows = 4" in stranded St st with larger needles, blocked

For pattern support, contact
annikaandreaknits@gmail.com

Notes:

This shawl is knitted as a traditional triangle shawl in stockinette stitch with a garter stitch border. The shawl is worked in 4 blocks of color which allows for endless combinations and the inclusion of all your favorite colors! Each block of color is transitioned to the next by a two-colored stranded section making this an interesting project to knit and to develop stranded knitting skills.

DIRECTIONS

Set-up

Using smaller needles and MC, CO 3 sts.
Rows 1-6: K.
After Row 6, do not turn work.
Rotate piece by 90 degrees and PU & K 3 sts from the side edge. 6 sts.
Rotate by 90 degrees again and PU & K 3 sts from CO edge. 9 sts.
Next Row: K3, (PM, P1) 3 times, PM, K3.

MC Section

This section is worked with MC only.
Row 1 (RS): K3, SM, M1L, K to next M, M1R, SM, K1, SM, M1L, K to next M, M1R, SM, K3. 4 sts inc.
Row 2: K3, SM, P to last M, SM, K3.
Repeat last 2 rows 25 more times. 113 sts.

MC and C1 Section

This section is worked with MC and C1 in stranded St st. The non-working yarn is carried on WS of work throughout this section.
Change to larger needles.
Row 1 (RS): K3 with MC, SM, M1L with MC, (K1 with C1, K1 with MC) to 1 st before M, K1 with C1, M1R with MC, SM, K1 with MC, SM, M1L with MC, (K1 with C1, K1 with MC) to 1 st before M, K1with C1, M1R with MC, SM, K3. 4 sts inc.
Row 2: K3 with MC, SM, P all sts to last M in the color they appear, SM, K3 with MC.
Row 3: K3 with MC, SM, M1L with C1, (K1 with MC, K1 with C1) to 1 st before M, K1 with MC, M1R with C1, SM, K1 with MC, SM, M1L with C1, (K1 with MC, K1 with C1) to 1 st before M, K1 with MC, M1R with C1, SM, K3 with MC. 4 sts inc.
Row 4: K3 with MC, SM, P all sts to last M in the color they appear, SM, K3 with MC.
Repeat last 4 rows 3 more times. 145 sts.
Break MC, leaving a 4" tail.

C1 Section

This section is worked with C1 only.
Change to smaller needles.
Row 1 (RS): K3, SM, M1L, K to next M, M1R, SM, K1, SM, M1L, K to next M, M1R, SM, K3. 4 sts inc.
Row 2: K3, SM, P to last M, SM, K3.
Repeat last 2 rows 25 more times. 249 sts

C1 and C2 Section

This section is worked with C1 and C2 in stranded St st. The non-working yarn is carried on WS of work throughout this section.
Change to larger needles.
Row 1 (RS): K3 with C1, SM, M1L with C1, (K1 with C2, K1 with C1) to 1 st before M, K1 with C2, M1R with C1, SM, K1 with C1, SM, M1L with C1, (K1 with C2, K1 with C1) to 1 st before M, K1with C2, M1R with C1, SM, K3. 4 sts inc.
Row 2: K3 with C1, SM, P all sts to last M in the color they appear, SM, K3 with C1.
Row 3: K3 with C1, SM, M1L with C2, (K1 with C1, K1 with C2) to 1 st before M, K1 with C1, M1R with C2, SM, K1 with C1, SM, M1L with C2, (K1 with C1, K1 with C2) to 1 st before M, K1 with C1, M1R with C2, SM, K3 with C1. 4 sts inc.
Row 4: K3 with C1, SM, P all sts to last M in the color they appear, SM, K3 with C1.
Repeat last 4 rows 3 more times. 281 sts.
Break C1, leaving a 4" tail.

C2 Section

This section is worked with C2 only.
Change to smaller needles.
Row 1 (RS): K3, SM, M1L, K to next M, M1R, SM, K1, SM, M1L, K to next M, M1R, SM, K3. 4 sts inc.
Row 2: K3, SM, P to last M, SM, K3.
Repeat last 2 rows 25 more times. 385 sts

C2 and C3 Section

This section is worked with C2 and C3 in stranded St st. The non-working yarn is carried on WS of work throughout this section.
Change to larger needles.
Row 1 (RS): K3 with C2, SM, M1L with C2, (K1 with C3, K1 with C2) to 1 st before M, K1 with C3, M1R with C2, SM, K1 with C2, SM, M1L with C2, (K1 with C3, K1 with C2) to 1 st before M, K1 with C3, M1R with C2, SM, K3. 4 sts inc.
Row 2: K3 with C2, SM, P all sts to last M in the color they appear, SM, K3 with C2.
Row 3: K3 with C2, SM, M1L with C3, (K1 with C2, K1 with C3) to 1 st before M, K1 with C2, M1R with C3, SM, K1 with C2, SM, M1L with C3, (K1 with C2, K1 with C3) to 1 st before M, K1 with C2, M1R with C3, SM, K3 with C2. 4 sts inc.
Row 4: K3 with C2, SM, P all sts to last M in the color they appear, SM, K3 with C2.
Repeat last 4 rows 3 more times. 417 sts.
Break C2, leaving a 4" tail.

C3 Section

This section is worked with C3 only.
Change to smaller needles.

Row 1 (RS): K3, SM, M1L, K to next M, M1R, SM, K1, SM, M1L, K to next M, M1R, SM, K3. 4 sts inc.
Row 2: K3, SM, P to last M, SM, K3.
Repeat last 2 rows 20 more times. 501 sts
Row 3: K3, SM, M1L, (P1, K1) to 1 before M, P1, M1R, SM, K1, SM, M1L, (P1, K1) to 1 before M, P1, M1R, SM, K3. 4 sts inc.
Row 4: K3, SM, (P1, K1) to 1 sts before M, P1, SM, P1, SM, (P1, K1) to 1 sts before M, P1, SM, K3.
Row 5: K3, SM, M1L P-wise, (K1, P1) to 1 before M, K1, M1R P-wise, SM, K1, SM, M1L P-wise, (K1, P1) to 1 before M, K1, M1R P-wise, SM, K3. 4 sts inc.
Row 6: K3, SM, (K1, P1) to 1 before M, K1, SM, P1, SM, (K1, P1) to 1 before M, K1, SM, K3.
Rep Rows 3-6 once more, then Rows 3-4 once more. 521 sts.
BO in pattern.

Finishing

Weave in ends, wash and block to measurements.

STRATOSPHERE

by Claire Slade

FINISHED MEASUREMENTS
76" wide x 22" deep

YARN
Knit Picks Hawthorne Multi
(80% Superwash Fine Highland Wool, 20% Polyamide (Nylon); 357 yards/100g); MC Cully 27416, C2 Portsmouth 27420, 1 skein each
Knit Picks Hawthorne Tonal Hand Paint
(80% Superwash Fine Highland Wool, 20% Polyamide (Nylon); 357 yards/100g): C1 Grants Pass 27408, 1 skein

NEEDLES
US 4 (3.5mm) straight or circular needles, or size to obtain gauge

NOTIONS
Yarn Needle

GAUGE
21 sts and 36 rows = 4" over garter st, blocked

For pattern support, contact
verilyknits@gmail.com

Notes:
This wedge-shaped shawl is knit from end to end in one piece, the pattern has three sections; color block section, stripe section and lace section.

Garter Body Pattern (worked flat)
Row 1 (RS): K to last st, KFB. 1 st inc.
Row 2 (WS): KFB, K to end. 1 st inc.
Row 3: K2tog, K to last st, KFB.
Row 4: KFB, K to end. 1 st inc.
Rep Rows 1-4 for pattern.

Lace Bind-off
K1, *K1, return the 2sts back to the left needle and K2tog TBL; rep from * to end.

Read the charts RS rows (odd numbers) from right to left, and WS rows (even numbers) from left to right.

DIRECTIONS

Color Block Section
Using MC CO 3 sts.
Work Rows 1-4 of Garter Body pattern 38 times. 117sts.

Stripe Section
Using MC work Rows 1-2 of Garter Body pattern.
Using C1 work Rows 3-4 of Garter Body pattern.
Rep last 4 rows 18 more times. 174sts.
Break MC.

Lace Section
Join C2 and work Rows 1-30 of Chart A. 197sts.
Work Rows 1-22 of Chart B. 213sts
BO all sts using the Lace BO.

Finishing
Weave in ends, wash and block by first pinning the shawl out into a triangle then pinning the lace section pulling the lace edge out in to gentle waves.

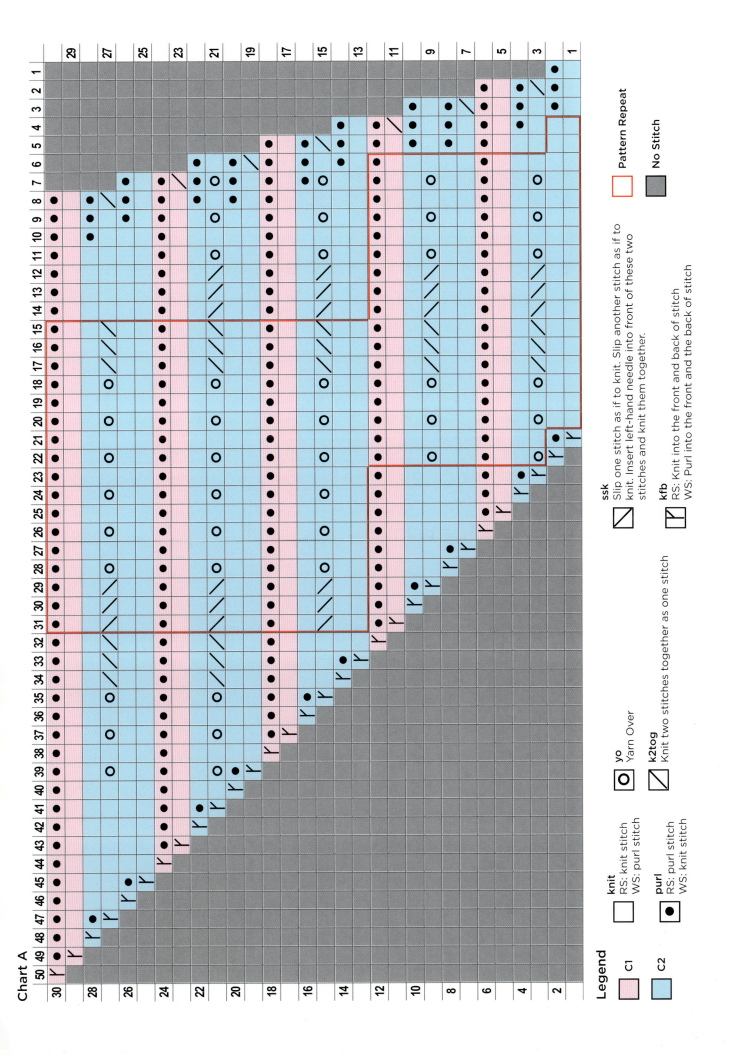

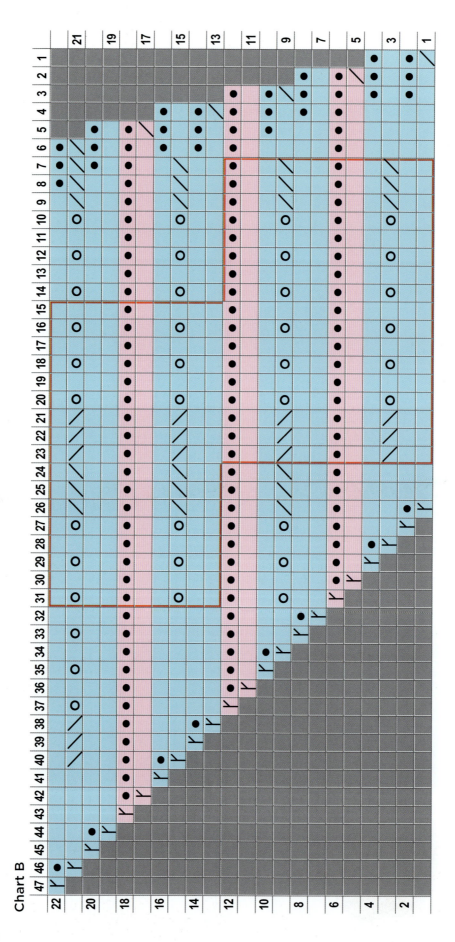

Chart B

WEST BLUFF

by Sierra Morningstar

FINISHED MEASUREMENTS
80" across wingspan x 24" at deepest point, blocked

YARN
Knit Picks Hawthorne Tonal Hand Paint (80%Superwash Fine Highland Wool, 20% Polyamide (Nylon); 357 yards/100g): C1 Astoria 27411, 1 skein; C3 Corvallis 27401, 2 skeins

Knit Picks Hawthorne Multi (80%Superwash Fine Highland Wool, 20% Polyamide (Nylon); 357 yards/100g): C2 Willamette 26866, 1 skein

NEEDLES
US 4 (3.5mm) 47" or longer circular needle, or size to obtain gauge

NOTIONS
Yarn Needle
Stitch Markers

GAUGE
24 sts and 36 rows = 4" in St st, blocked

For pattern support, contact Morn5420@yahoo.com

Notes:

West Bluff is a crescent shawl knit from the top down, shaped by increases on every row. The pattern alternates between plain Stockinette Stitch, Stockinette Stripes, and a simple Mesh Lace Pattern.

Stockinette Stitch Pattern (worked flat)
Row 1 (RS): K3, SM, M1R, K to M, M1L, SM, K3.
Row 2 (WS): K3, SM, M1LP, P to M, M1RP, SM, K3.
Rep Rows 1 & 2 for pattern.

Mesh Lace (worked flat)
Row 1 (RS): K3, SM, M1R, K1, (YO, Sl-K2-PSSO) to 1 st before M, K1, M1L, SM, K3.
Row 2 and every WS Row: K3, SM, M1LP, P to M, M1RP, SM, K3.
Row 3: K3, SM, M1R, K1, (YO, Sl-K2-PSSO) to 2 sts before M, K1, M1L, SM, K3.
Row 5: K3, SM, M1R, K2, (YO, Sl-K2-PSSO) to 2 sts before M, K1, M1L, SM, K3.
Row 7: K3, SM, M1R, K2, (YO, Sl-K2-PSSO) to M, K1, M1L, SM, K3.
Row 9: K3, SM, M1R, (YO, Sl-K2-PSSO) to M, M1L, SM, K3.
Row 11: K3, SM, M1R, (YO, Sl-K2-PSSO) to 1 st before M, K1, M1L, SM, K3.
Rep Rows 1-12 for pattern.

If using the chart, read the charts RS rows (odd numbers) from right to left, and WS rows (even numbers) from left to right.

Elastic Bind Off
Step 1: K 2.
Step 2: Insert LH needle in front of two sts just worked, K these 2 sts tog TBL.
Step 3: K1.
Rep Steps 2 & 3 until there is 1 st left on LH needle.
Step 4: K1, K 2 sts on right-hand needle tog TBL.
Cut yarn and thread through last loop.

Make 1 Left (M1L): With LH needle, pick up the horizontal strand running between sts from the front; K into the back of loop.
Make 1 Right (M1R): With LH needle, pick up the horizontal strand running between sts from the back; K into the front of loop.
Make 1 Left Purl (M1LP): With LH needle, pick up the horizontal strand running between sts from the front; P into the back of loop.
Make 1 Right Purl (M1RP): With LH needle, pick up the horizontal strand running between sts from the back, P into the front of loop.
Slip 1, Knit 2, Pass Slipped Stitch Over (Sl-K2-PSSO): Sl 1, K2, pass the slipped st over the K2.

DIRECTIONS
Garter Tab Cast On
With C1 CO 3 sts.
K 32 rows.
Row 33: K3, turn work 90 degrees, PU & K 16 sts from side of work, turn work 90 degrees again, PU & K 3 sts from CO edge. 22 sts

Shawl
Set-Up Row
K3, PM, P to last 3 sts, PM, K3.

Work 16 reps of Stockinette Stitch Pattern. 86 sts.
Work 2 reps of Mesh Lace Pattern. Work Rows 1-10 once more. 154 sts.

With C2, work 1 rep of Stockinette Stitch Pattern.
With C1, work 1 rep of Stockinette Stitch Pattern.
Rep last 4 rows 2 more times. 178 sts.
Cut C1.

With C2, work 16 reps of Stockinette Stitch Pattern. 242 sts.
Work 2 reps of Mesh Lace Pattern. Work Rows 1-10 once more. 310 sts.

With C3, work 1 rep of Stockinette Stitch Pattern.
With C2, work 1 rep of Stockinette Stitch Pattern.
Rep last 4 rows 2 more times. 334 sts.
Cut C2.

With C3, work 16 reps of Stockinette Stitch Pattern. 398 sts.
Work 2 reps of Mesh Lace Pattern. Work rows 1-10 once more. 466 sts.

BO using the Elastic Bind Off.

Finishing
Weave in ends, wet block to measurements.

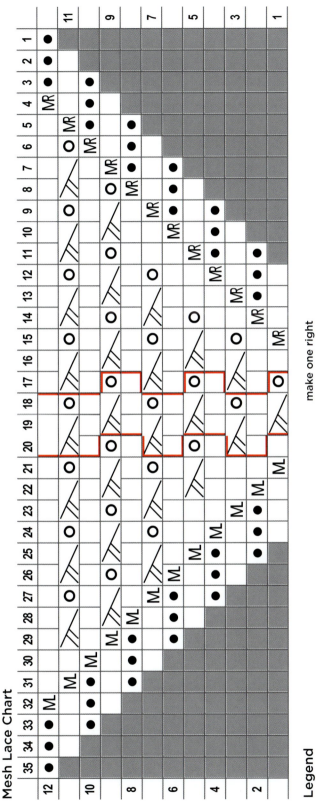

WILD VORTEX SHAWL

by Mone Dräger

FINISHED MEASUREMENTS
56" wide along top edge, 28" deep

YARN
Knit Picks Preciosa Tonal Fingering
Yarn (100% Merino Wool; 437 yards/100g): C1 Maritime 26941, C2 Pokeberry 26953, C3 Canary 26945; 1 skein each

NEEDLES
US 4 (3.5mm) 32" or longer circular needle to accommodate the large number of stitches, or size to obtain gauge

NOTIONS
Yarn Needle
Stitch Markers

GAUGE
18 sts and 32 rows = 4" in Garter stitch, blocked
20 sts and 26 rows = 4" Wild Vortex Border pattern, blocked

For pattern support, contact
mone.draeger@gmx.de

Notes:

Like a vortex in the sea, the wedges of this shawl seem to spin around an invisible axis. The three-colored shawl is knit from the top down, with two wedges in each color, forming the shape of three quarters circle. The main part is worked in garter stitch, the edging is a simple lace pattern which results in a curvy edge, enhancing the idea of a vortex.

The shawl is knit using all three colors in one row, the joins between the different colored segments are made invisible by interlocking the working yarns.

Wild Vortex Border Pattern
(worked flat over a multiple of 17 sts)
Row 1 (RS): K.
Row 2 (WS): P.
Row 3: (K2tog) 3 times, (YO, K1) 5 times, YO, (SSK) 3 times.
Row 4: P.
Row 5: K.
Rows 6-9: Rep Rows 2-5.
Rows 10-12: K.
Rep Rows 1-12 for pattern.

Color Changes
The shawl is worked using all three colors in one row. To avoid holes at the color changes, always interlock the yarns. The old color is always brought over the new color; then the new color is picked up from under the old color and worked from there. On RS rows, knit to the color change, leave the working yarn at the back above the new color and pick up the new color from under the old color and knit to next color change. On WS rows, knit to the color change, bring the working yarn between the needles to the front (the side facing you), place it above the new color and pick up the new color from under the old color and bring it between the needles to the back. Knit to next color change. A tutorial can be found here: http://tutorials.knitpicks.com/intarsia/.

DIRECTIONS

Garter Stitch Body
With C1, CO 4 sts; with C2, CO 4 sts; with C3, CO 4 sts. 12 sts.
Set-up Row (WS): With C3, *K2, PM, K2; rep from * once using C2, then rep once more using C1.
Row 1 (RS): With C1, * K1, YO, K to M, SM, K1, YO, K to last st in working color; rep from * once using C2, then rep once more using C3. 6 sts inc.
Row 2 (WS): With C3, *K to 2 sts before M, K1 TBL, K1, SM, K to last 2 sts in working color, K1 TBL, K1; rep from * once using C2, then rep once more using C1.
Rep last two rows 79 more times. Remove M on last row. 492 sts; 164 sts in each color.

Lace Border
Set-up Row 1 (RS): With C1, K1, YO, K3, YO, (K4, YO) 39 times, K3, YO, K1, with C2, (K4, YO) 40 times, K4, with C3, K1, YO, K3, YO, (K4, YO) 39 times, K3, YO, K1. 616 sts; 206 sts in C1, 204 sts in C2, 206 sts in C3.
Set-up Row 2 (WS): With C3, K1, K1 TBL, K3, (K1 TBL, K4) 39 times, K1 TBL, K3, K1 TBL, K1, with C2, K4, (K1 TBL, K4) 40 times, with C1, K1, K1 TBL, K3, (K1 TBL, K4) 39 times, K1 TBL, K3, K1 TBL, K1.
Row 1 (RS): With C1, K2, work Wild Vortex Border pattern 12 times across to color change; with C2, work Wild Vortex Border pattern 12 times across to next color change; with C3, work Wild Vortex Border pattern 12 times across to last 2 sts, K2.
Row 2 (WS): With C3, K2, work as established in Wild Vortex Border pattern and using the appropriate color to last 2 sts, K2. Repeat last 2 rows until Rows 1-12 of the Wild Vortex Border pattern have been worked 4 times.
BO as follows: K1, *K1, return both sts to LH needle, K2tog TBL; rep from * to end. Break yarn and pull through remaining st.

Finishing
Weave in ends, wash and block to measurements.

Wild Vortex Border Chart

	17	16	15	14	13	12	11	10	9	8	7	6	5	4	3	2	1	
12	●	●	●	●	●	●	●	●	●	●	●	●	●	●	●	●	●	
																		11
10	●	●	●	●	●	●	●	●	●	●	●	●	●	●	●	●	●	
																		9
8																		
	\	\	\	O		O		O		O		O		O	/	/	/	7
6																		
																		5
4																		
	\	\	\	O		O		O		O		O		O	/	/	/	3
2																		
																		1

Legend

☐ **knit**
RS: knit stitch
WS: purl stitch

● **purl**
RS: purl stitch
WS: knit stitch

O **yo**
Yarn Over

╲ **k2tog**
Knit two stitches together as one stitch

╲ **ssk**
Slip one stitch as if to knit. Slip another stitch as if to knit. Insert left-hand needle into front of these two stitches and knit them together.

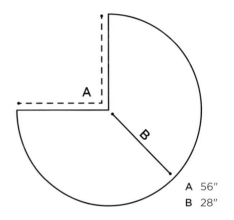

A 56"
B 28"

Abbreviations

BO	bind off	**KFB**	knit into the front and back of stitch	**PU**	pick up	**SSP**	sl, sl, p these 2 sts tog tbl
BOR	beginning of round	**K-wise**	knitwise	**P-wise**	purlwise	**SSSK**	sl, sl, sl, k these 3 sts tog
cn	cable needle	**LH**	left hand	**rep**	repeat	**St st**	stockinette stitch
CC	contrast color	**M**	marker	**Rev St st**	reverse stockinette stitch	**sts**	stitch(es)
CDD	Centered double dec	**M1**	make one stitch	**RH**	right hand	**TBL**	through back loop
CO	cast on	**M1L**	make one left-leaning stitch	**rnd(s)**	round(s)	**TFL**	through front loop
cont	continue	**M1R**	make one right-leaning stitch	**RS**	right side	**tog**	together
dec	decrease(es)	**MC**	main color	**Sk**	skip	**W&T**	wrap & turn (see specific instructions in pattern)
DPN(s)	double pointed needle(s)	**P**	purl	**Sk2p**	sl 1, k2tog, pass slipped stitch over k2tog: 2 sts dec	**WE**	work even
EOR	every other row	**P2tog**	purl 2 sts together	**SKP**	sl, k, psso: 1 st dec	**WS**	wrong side
inc	increase	**PM**	place marker	**SL**	slip	**WYIB**	with yarn in back
K	knit	**PFB**	purl into the front and back of stitch	**SM**	slip marker	**WYIF**	with yarn in front
K2tog	knit two sts together	**PSSO**	pass slipped stitch over	**SSK**	sl, sl, k these 2 sts tog	**YO**	yarn over

Knit Picks®

Knit Picks yarn is both luxe and affordable—a seeming contradiction trounced! But it's not just about the pretty colors; we also care deeply about fiber quality and fair labor practices, leaving you with a gorgeously reliable product you'll turn to time and time again.

THIS COLLECTION FEATURES

Hawthorne Multi
Fingering Weight
80% Superwash Fine Highland Wool, 20% Polyamide (Nylon)

Hawthorne Kettle Dye
Fingering Weight
80% Superwash Fine Highland Wool, 20% Polyamide (Nylon)

Hawthorne Tonal Hand Paint
Fingering Weight
80% Superwash Fine Highland Wool, 20% Polyamide (Nylon)

Hawthorne Speckle Hand Paint
Fingering Weight
80% Superwash Fine Highland Wool, 20% Polyamide (Nylon)

Stroll Sock Yarn
Fingering Weight
75% Superwash Merino Wool, 25% Nylon

Stroll Hand Painted Sock Yarn
Fingering Weight
75% Superwash Merino Wool, 25% Nylon

Stroll Tonal Sock Yarn
Fingering Weight
75% Superwash Merino Wool, 25% Nylon

Stroll Gradient Sock Yarn
Fingering Weight
75% Superwash Merino Wool, 25% Nylon

Preciosa Tonal
Fingering Weight
75% Superwash Merino Wool, 25% Nylon

Gloss
Fingering Weight
70% Merino Wool, 30% Silk

View these beautiful yarns and more at www.KnitPicks.com